Praise for

four small words

I've been waiting for this book for a long time. Jarrett Stevens does more with four words than most people are able to accomplish with an entire book. My four words are simple, "Buy this book today!"

—JON ACUFF, *New York Times* Bestselling Author of *Do Over: Rescue Monday, Reinvent Your Work, and Never Get Stuck*

Jarret is both a longtime friend and terrific communicator. Blessed is the reader who can sit at his feet.

—JOHN ORTBERG, Senior Pastor of Menlo Park Presbyterian Church in California and Author of *All the Places to Go*

Years ago, Jarrett and I worked together, which meant I was lucky enough to hear him teach hundreds of times. His teaching made complicated things simple, and his love for God's word was contagious. I'm so happy to report that this book captures the very best of his teaching—that same ability to distill easily tangled concepts into clear and meaningful insights, and that spirit of warmth and invitation.

—SHAUNA NIEQUIST, Author of *Bread & Wine; Bittersweet;* and *Cold Tangerines*

There are so many different tools and thoughts on how to understand Scripture better. However, the combination of Jarrett's storytelling and knowledge on how to study the Bible is such a refreshing take on a crucial skill. Everyone should read this important work.

—TYLER REAGIN, Executive Director of Catalyst, A Community of Change Makers

four small words

four small words

A SIMPLE WAY TO
UNDERSTAND THE BIBLE

JARRETT STEVENS

ZONDERVAN

Four Small Words
Copyright © 2015 by Jarrett Stevens

This title is also available as a Zondervan ebook. Visit www.zondervan.com/ebooks.

Requests for information should be addressed to:
Zondervan, 3900 *Sparks Drive SE, Grand Rapids, Michigan 49546*

Library of Congress Cataloging-in-Publication Data

Stevens, Jarrett.
    Four small words : a simple way to understand the Bible / Jarrett Stevens.
        p. cm.
    ISBN 978-0-310-27115-4 (pbk.) - ISBN 978-0-310-56346-4 (ebook) -
    ISBN 978-0-310-06614-9 (mobile app)
    1. Bible - Hermeneutics. 2. Bible - Criticism, interpretation, etc. 3. Bible -
Reading. I. Title.
    BS476.S765   2015
    220.6 - dc23   2015025681

Cover design: Faceout Studio
Interior design: Kait Lamphere

First printing October 2015 / Printed in the United States of America

I dedicate this book to our amazing children, Elijah and Gigi.

The two of you are our greatest source of joy and our
greatest reminder of God's goodness and love.

Your mom and I love how the two of you
love God and love his story.

Thank you for cheering your daddy on to write this book.

I'm so proud to be your daddy.

I love you heart and soul.

And I dedicate this book to Soul City Church.

You are my people.

Your stories fill the pages of this book and
are forever a part of my story.

Thank you for giving me so many reasons to write.

It's unbelievable to consider all that God has done,
all that he is doing, and all that is to come.

Only God!

contents

Bible versions

acknowledgments

Thank you to my wife, Jeanne, for your belief, support, encouragement, and patience as God worked this book out in me. You are my partner in every sense of the word. I love you heart and soul.

Thank you to my editor, Carolyn McCready, for holding me to the vision of this book and not letting me settle for anything less. Thank you for pushing me, for being patient with me, and for partnering with me in this endeavor.

Deepest gratitude to Elizabeth Marshall for helping me find this book in the midst of many piles of pages. You brought clarity and direction and helped me to befriend the delete button. I simply could not have done this without you.

I'd like to thank Londa Alderink and her team at Zondervan for their belief in this book and their desire to get it into as many hands as possible. Your creativity and commitment to people's spiritual growth are inspiring.

And thanks as well to Jim Ruark for making sure that every "i" was dotted and every "t" was crossed. Thank you for all your work to make sure that my voice and the message of this book came through with care and clarity.

Thank you to the Elders of Soul City Church who empower, encourage, and expect me to use my God-given gifts to their fullest and truest potential. Thank you for how you loved, cared, and carried me through this book.

And lastly, I want to thank my first grade Sunday school teacher, Mrs. Dopart. Thank you for giving me my very first Bible. You planted a seed in me that has borne fruit throughout every season of my life.

4

Part One

introduction

God's Big (Small) Idea

One Big Idea. Four Small Words.

Let's be honest: The Bible is not an easy book to read. It's one complete work broken into two distinct parts, containing 66 different books written by 40 unique writers over the period of 1,600 years! It was written in several different styles: biographical accounts, historical accounts, poetry, wisdom writings, prophecy, personal letters, and letters to churches. It was originally written in three different languages: Hebrew, Aramaic, and Greek. And it has been translated into more languages than any other book in human history.

This is a book that has been printed roughly six billion times (and that is before it became an app!). It is a book that wars have been waged over, and a book used to bring peace. A book read at the inauguration of presidents and the coronation of kings, and a book read at the execution of death-row inmates. It is a book that has been the source text for much of humanity for the last 3,500 years. It is a book so complex that people have dedicated their life's work to studying it, and yet so simple that even a child can understand it.

As if all of its unique features weren't enough to contribute to its complexity, the content itself can at times be ... well ... quite complex. Outside of the eyewitness accounts of those involved in the events of the Bible and the oral history that echoed after them, the Bible is one of the primary ways that God conveys His message to the world. Some verses are so deeply layered with transformational truth that some 2,000 years later they are still a mystery yet (if ever) to be fully understood. There are books and chapters and verses and even single words that are to this day held up like a precious gem, each turn revealing a fresh reflection on God and us. This is no ordinary book.

My Name in Gold

Do you remember the first time you came into contact with a Bible? I do. I remember my very first Bible. I got it when I was seven. It was a gift from my Sunday school teacher—Mrs. Dopart. She got a Bible for each of the kids in our Sunday school class. What made Mrs. Dopart a cut above the average Sunday school teacher was that she had my name engraved in gold letters on the front of the Bible. Gold letters! Do you realize how big of a deal that is to a little guy? It made me feel so special. And I always knew that if times got tough, I could burn the Bible and melt down those gold letters to cover the cost of my next *Star Wars* action figure.

My gold-laden Bible was more like a "mini-Bible." It was just the New Testament and was small enough to fit into the back pocket of my Toughskins Jeans. It was a sweet gift considering that I was *just* learning how to read, and it was of course written in King James English. Needless to say, I doth not read it much. But it did have pictures. Those illustrations were my visual cue to the Bible. I would look at every detail and try to fill in the blanks as best a seven-year-old could, figuring out what the "story" of the Bible was. I needed those pictures. I needed those cues. I needed help, because even though mine was merely a "mini-Bible," it was still a very big book. With huge concepts and confusing context, that would prove to be a lifelong pursuit to seek to understand and apply. I still have that Bible to this day.

Years later, for my eighth-grade graduation, I received an NIV Study Bible. While this one didn't come with any gold engravings, it did come with a Bible cover of fine Corinthian leather. The tan on brown cover came with a large sword stitched into the front and some sort of marsupial pouch on the back to hold notes or pencils or younglings; I was never quite sure what to do with that. This Bible had both Testaments this time. Not only that, but this Bible had notes and commentary and color maps, and the all-important chart of weights and measurements in the back! I would fill that Bible with personal notes, highlights, and sermon notes. I used that Bible all the way through college. It was my workhorse Bible and a sort of chronicle of my spiritual growth. I still have that Bible to this day.

While I was very fortunate to be given the gift of these two Bibles, the gift that I realize now that I most needed was the gift of understanding. I learned how to read the Bible at a young age. I learned how to memorize its verses. I learned how to find things on its maps, I learned how to convert shekels to dollars ... but I didn't have an understanding of how it all fit together. I didn't understand the bigger picture. I didn't understand how the stories related to one another, and if I'm being honest, I didn't understand how they applied to my life. I gained knowledge, but lacked understanding.

At last count, I have somewhere around thirty Bibles on various bookshelves around my home and office. Yet, it doesn't matter how many Bibles I own, or how big or small they are, whether they're for adults or for our kids; this book is still the most unique, honest, challenging, comforting, and yes, sometimes most confusing book I've ever read. It somehow continues to give answers to my biggest questions while stirring up questions to some of my most confidently assumed answers. The more I get to know it, the more it opens itself up to me. Stories I've heard a hundred times before still sound fresh and new. There are parts of the Bible that continue to challenge me. There are parts that still frustrate me. There are parts that still confuse me. And yet ... all these years later I am still engaging this book, and it is still engaging me.

And that's exactly what *this* book is about. This book is meant to help you understand, engage, and love that book. This book is not about more knowledge, but rather about finding a greater and richer understanding of the Bible. An understanding that draws you into a transformational relationship with the God who gave it to you.

Access > Interest

Not surprisingly, more and more people in Western culture are reading the Bible less and less these days. Fifty years ago the Bible was the book on just about everyone's shelf, even if it was collecting dust. Today it too often can't be found on the shelf at all. Never before in Western culture have we had greater access to the Bible and seemingly less interest in it. There is really nothing left that would keep someone from finding, having or reading a Bible ... except for their personal resistance or presumed sense of irrelevance.

While there are people in parts of Iraq, Afghanistan, China, and North Korea who would give their lives for a Bible, Western culture doesn't really seem to be as moved or motivated. In fact, in 2014 the Barna Group (in partnership with the American Bible Society) found that while 88 percent of Americans own a Bible (a high percentage), only 33 percent actually claim to read their Bible once a week or more (a low percentage).

However, we are experiencing a different story at Soul City Church in Chicago. My wife and I are the pastors there, and when we started the church in the fall of 2010, we noticed that every time we asked people to open their Bibles to a certain book and chapter, the majority of those gathered didn't have Bibles with them. Even with those who did, there was hesitancy in knowing where to turn. So we decided to stock every seat with a Bible, with the open invitation that if you didn't own a Bible, the Bible that you were now holding was yours! Go ahead ... take it. Steal a Bible from church. People laugh every time we say it like that, but since we began our "Steal a Bible" program, hundreds and hundreds of Bibles have been "stolen" from our church. It is a divine delight every time we have to place another order for more Bibles.

One of our "Stolen Bible" stories comes from my friend Joe. Not too long ago, I was sitting across the table from Joe at an Irish pub in the middle of the afternoon. His wife of nine months had recently been diagnosed with stage four lung cancer. They were obviously in a state of shock. His wife, in his words, was a person of faith, but he

was not fully on board with it all yet. He was quick to tell me, however, that she had something that they both needed—a connection
to God. She had a faith that he believed could carry them through
this difficult season. He wanted it and was asking me where to begin.

I asked him if he had ever read the Bible.

"Not really!" he replied. "I tried recently. I started in the beginning part, but got real confused and real bored real quick."

I asked if he would like to read it in a different way, a way that
might actually make more sense. Without hesitation he told me he
would. I told him about this idea of Four Small Words and how every
part of the Bible is a part of a bigger story—even the confusing and
boring parts. I directed him to the gospel of Mark because it's the
shortest gospel and moves the fastest. I told him that I would check
in and see how it was going over the next couple weeks and that we
could connect after he got back from a month-long treatment cycle for
his wife. We prayed a short prayer—the kind you pray at Irish pubs in
the middle of the day—and he was on his way, taking the first couple
steps into a book that I pray he pursues for the rest of his life.

Joe and I got back together a few months later, and it was evident
that he was on a growth tear. He was doing whatever he had to do to
grow in his newly forming relationship with God—including reading the Bible. We reconnected over lunch and got into all that he
was learning, wondering, and wrestling with spiritually. Eventually
in our conversation we got to the Holy Spirit and what happens and
what is possible when God lives *in* us. In a sense of genuine wonder
and bewilderment, Joe quickly looked around the room and leaned
slightly in and asked, "Do other people know about this? This seems
like some Secret Society Stuff!" We laughed at the thought of that . . .
and then I taught him the secret handshake and swore him to secrecy.

What I think Joe was really asking in that moment wasn't "Do
other people know about this?" but rather, "How come more people
don't live like this?" How come people don't live more in a way that
reflects that they understand and actually believe the teachings of
the Bible?

You see, I believe that there is a genuine hunger and desire for a truth that is greater than us. I believe that's why you picked up this book. What if instead of feeling intimidated by the Bible, you could be inspired by it? What if your understanding actually led to a deeper and more sincere belief and faith? I think it is more possible than you know.

From 774,000 to 4

When it comes to the Bible, it's easy to feel like a Freshman Scrub player stepping into a varsity league of people who know the Bible more than you do. These are people who own multiple copies of the Bible; have elaborate systems of pens, highlighters, and notes in their Bibles; and even have parts of it memorized. This feeds our intimidation and reluctance more than we may even realize.

Awhile back, I was driving home from a late night of doing something or other and while flipping through stations on my car radio, I stumbled across a Christian program. The host of the show was apparently a very intelligent Bible expert whom ordinary "non-expert" people like you and me can call up and ask difficult, deep, or confusing questions about the Bible. I was amazed at this guy's knowledge. He was like a Bible black belt.

What interested me was not his quick and effortless answers to every caller's difficult questions, but rather the pre-defeated tone of the people who called in. Without exception there was a sense of frustration and desperation in their voices. These were big questions. Questions that had inevitably stumped them. Questions that came from conversations with family, friends, or coworkers that obviously didn't end well (or else they wouldn't be calling in at 10:47 p.m.). In their voices I heard the familiar emotion that I feel whenever I'm around a Bible black belt. It's a feeling that maybe you have felt when it seems as if a pastor is preaching past your pay grade, or when you simply sit down to read the Bible by yourself. It's the feeling that when it comes to the Bible, you just don't know *enough*.

Since its original printing in 1456, there have been hundreds of thousands of books written *about* the Bible. Countless volumes of books explore in depth the meaning of almost every single word in the text. No other single source text in our human history has had as many words written about it as the Bible. So if you have ever felt that you don't know "enough" about the Bible, the truth is ... you don't. You can't. But what if that's not really the point?

What if God's idea behind the Bible isn't the endless pursuit of *knowing enough*, but rather *understanding more?* There's a big difference between knowing and understanding. Knowing is a left-brain thing — the objective acquisition of countless data points that are stored away for later reference. Understanding, however, is something completely different. It is the stuff of the right-brain. Understanding is seeing the bigger picture, being able to connect the dots, to see the forest through the mass of endless trees, to see the story through the mass of endless words. It can take a lifetime of studying words until you feel as if you *know* something, but you can *understand* something in far fewer words ... like, say, four.

I believe that the story of God can be best understood in the context of four main movements or parts. These are the four small words that give us the big idea of the Bible: *Of, Between, With,* and *In.*

1. **OF** — Creation — The Story of Our True Identity (Genesis 1–2)
2. **BETWEEN** — The Old Testament — The Story of Separation (Genesis 3 — Malachi 4)
3. **WITH** — The Gospels — The Story of a Present God (Matthew 1 — Acts 1)
4. **IN** — The Rest of the New Testament — The Story of a People Inhabited by God (Acts 2 — Revelation 22)

Not only do these words tell the linear, chronological story of the Bible, but at a much deeper level they resonate with each of our own stories. As you will see through the course of this book, these four small words tell your story and my story as well.

1. **OF**—Each of us is created with an identity that comes from God and is so much bigger than who we are right now.
2. **BETWEEN**—Each of us has experienced separation from God when sin comes between us in one season or another.
3. **WITH**—Each of us has had moments when we felt "close" to God, when we knew He was with us, or when we desired that feeling
4. **IN**—Each of us has been created to live with the power and presence of God in us in our everyday lives.

Four small words that not only reveal the bigger picture of the story of the Bible, but also give you a picture of what your story *is* and *can be* with God.

Again, this book isn't about knowing more; rather, it's about understanding better. This book is about connecting the dots and seeing the overarching story through all the words. It is not an attempt to add more, but to make more sense of what you may already know. It's for those of us who may have heard the stories before, but have missed the bigger story. And that is not just the story of God, but your story too, for in that bigger story we find our own small but significant stories. Only when we begin to understand the bigger story can we hope to understand our own story.

So throughout this book we will weave back and forth between the story of God and the story of us. The front section of each chapter is focused on how that specific small word plays out within the context of that section of the Bible. Through the use of specific biblical passages, stories, and examples you will be able to connect the dots of the larger theme through its specific small word. The back section of each chapter is all about personal application. In other words, how does each small word have big implications on your everyday, ordinary life? How can you begin to connect the dots between the four major movements found in the story of the Bible and the ever-unfolding story of your life?

So before we continue, I ask you to do two things:

(1) Ask God to illuminate your mind and open your heart. Ask
    Him to meet with you as you engage His story and yours
    in a fresh and transformational way. And ask Him to help
    connect the dots between His book and your life.

    You can pray that prayer right now! Go ahead ... I'll wait.

(2) Have a Bible close by when reading—whether it's on your
    phone, tablet, or good old ink and paper. It's important that
    you do the work of connecting the dots for yourself. As I cite
    references and stories from the Bible, look them up. See for
    yourself. See if you can find *more* connections. Let this book
    and that Book truly work together. I believe the growth that
    will come out of it will be nothing less than transformational!

My Hope for You

I have spent the last few years of my life working on this book.
All along the way, I have been praying for you. That might sound
strange, because we don't really know each other. But I have been
praying that whatever words God gives me would be a gift to you.
I've been praying that this book might "reframe" your understanding
of the Bible and how it reveals God's love for you and for the world.
I've been praying that this book would ignite a deeper desire in you
to actually *know* this God of the Bible, not just know *about* Him.

My hope for you is that you will find yourself not only in the
pages of this book, but in the pages of *that* book. That the story of
God as found in the Bible would become *your* story. That you would
read it differently. That you would share it more personally. That you
would give up on *knowing enough* and begin to *understand* what it is
that God has been communicating to you and this world for the last
two thousand years.

Now, without any further ado, let's get into the Words!

4

Part Two

OF

Genesis 1—3

The Big Idea of the Small Word: OF

The first of the four small words in the story of God is the word OF.

Our understanding of the word OF comes from two basic concepts:

(1) Coming From
(2) Belonging To

For example, the title of the book *The Adventures of Tom Sawyer* by Mark Twain means that these adventures *come from* the life of Tom Sawyer and belong to his story (including the part where he sings in church about all his favorite "fights" in the Bible).

You intuitively know that the phrase "the United States OF America" is how you describe all of the separate states that *come from* the forming of our nation and *belong* to our country (including the Nation State of Texas).

Strictly biologically, we can understand the concept of OF. Each of us physically *comes from* two others. No one magically appears from nothing. Forty-two years ago Steve and Jeneanne Stevens came together, and I *came from* them. Not only do I *come from* them, but there are also parts of me that *belong to* them. Through the miraculous act of conception, God "copy and pasted" parts of their DNA into me. Those parts of me are undeniably "me," but they are inextricably connected to "them." Make sense?

Interestingly enough, this same biological concept is also theological. Genesis 1 and 2 tell us that we don't just come from or belong to *something*, but rather, we come from and belong to *Someone*. Your identity comes from and belongs to another identity … bigger than your parents. It has a source. It has a beginning. It has meaning. We see this in the first few paragraphs of the Bible.

> Then God said, "Let us make human beings in our image, in our likeness." …
> So God created human beings in his own image,
> in the image of God he created them;
> male and female he created them. (Gen. 1:26–27 TNIV)

The story of the Creation is the story of our beginning. It begins with humanity being OF God. Simply defined: Each of us comes from God and belongs to God. Whether or not you believe that yet, whether or not you can understand its deep spiritual significance, the Bible begins with the fact that you come from and belong to your Creator God. If you are ever going to make sense of your story, you have to start here. If you are ever going to answer the questions of identity and purpose, you have to start with the One whom you are *of*.

God, in His infinite wisdom and deliberate design, decided to deposit in you and me a glimpse of Himself. He gave a divine sense of dignity in forming both men and women to be bearers of Himself. Your mere existence is meant to remind you and declare to this world that each of us comes from Him and belongs to Him. And God, knowing how significant this is and how often we would forget this, decided to write glimpses of Himself into His creation.

Thomas Merton in his *New Seeds of Contemplation* wrote that

> God utters me like a word containing a partial thought of himself. A word will never be able to comprehend the voice that utters it. But if I am true to the concept God utters in me, if I am true to the thought in him I was meant to embody, I shall be full of his actuality and find him everywhere in myself, and find myself nowhere.
> I shall be lost in him.[1]

---

1. Thomas Merton, *New Seeds of Contemplation* (reprint, New York: New Directions Publications, 2007).

This is a quote that I committed to memory many years ago, strictly because of how often I forget this all-important truth. There is intentionality in my identity. There is a purpose to my person. I am a glimpse of God,... and so are you!

In the opening lines of the story, God gave Adam and Eve a glimpse of Himself that would serve as a reminder to them and to us that there is a God whose image we bear. A God whose image serves as a reminder of who He is and a compass as to whom He intends us to be. You are the *exhalo Dei*—the exhale of God. The natural outpouring of a supernatural God. A reflection of His perfection. You did not just "get here"; you were lovingly placed here by God, His fingerprints still all over you. God gives us glimpses of His glory found in the contours of His creation. To know the One that you are OF is to know the one that you are meant to BE. This is where the story of God begins. This is where your story begins. You are OF God.

As simple as it sounds, this idea is incredibly important to sit with. If your world is anything like mine, it is filled with a thousand different messages of who you are and who you are supposed to be. It is filled with spoken and unspoken expectations and even demands for you to be something, anything, other than who you are created to be. Your identity in and of God is both your compass and rudder for navigating the vast and wild waters of this world. If you lose who you are OF, you lose who you are. Your identity in God is simultaneously where you are going *and* how you get there. In other words, it's not only about *who* you are becoming, but *how* you are becoming who you are.

Who you are in God defines who you are as a friend, a spouse, a father, a mother, a son, a daughter, an employee, a boss. It defines those things—and not the other way around. So much of my life has been a response or reaction to others. A response to what others expected of me, loved about me, disliked about me, or didn't understand about me. Most of it was well intended; some of it was not. Most of it was unspoken; some of it was not. But all of it went into the pot of who I thought I was supposed to be, based on what others could see. From how I dressed, to the music I listened to, to the sports I played and didn't play, to the college I chose, and the major I declared. Rather than *living from*, I *responded to*. Maybe you can relate to that.

This is why knowing who you are OF matters so much. If you don't start here, you will end up just about anywhere but where you're supposed to be. You will be just about anyone but who you're created to be. So ... do you know the source of your soul? Do you know the truth of where your story and identity begin? Do you know the One that you are of? If you ever hope to know who you are and what you're meant to do in this world, you must start here. You must start with OF.

It's Not Where You're At, It's Where You're From

It's an odd thing to be so close to home and yet not know where you're from, to try and move forward without knowing where you're coming from.

When I was fifteen years old, my family moved to a new house across town. The house was fine—closer to work for my mom, closer to my friends, closer to school—but what excited me most about our new house had nothing to do with the house at all. It was the hill that the street was on, a hill that came down and leveled out right in front of our house. As a skateboarder, I felt as though it were my duty to stake my claim on that treacherous peak! So, days after moving in, with my parents both at work, I unpacked my skateboard and walked up to the top of that hill. In hindsight, I can concede that perhaps I should have worn protective pads or a helmet. Perhaps I should have had some buddies with me. Perhaps I should have actually learned our new address and phone number. But I was fifteen, and those were minor details for small-minded people who didn't have a giant hill beckoning them to leave their mark on it ... literally.

With a small push, I was off. About a third of the way down the hill, I realized that I was way out of my league. By two-thirds of the way down, I realized that I was way out of control. And by the bottom of the hill, I was just out. Breaking what I was sure was the land speed record for James Avenue, I lost control of my board and rode over a manhole cover, which threw me off of my board and onto my head. With blood beginning to make its way down the back of my head and onto my shirt, I did what any gnarly teenage skater would do: I screamed like a nine-year-old girl. A neighbor who witnessed the whole thing and heard the scream assumed the worst and called 911.

When the fire truck and ambulance arrived, they began to check my level of consciousness. I answered the basics: name, date, etc. But when they asked what my address was, I was stumped. "Uhhhh...." When they asked my phone number, I had the same dumbfounded response: "Ummm ... 510 .... uhhh." I was only fifty yards from our new house—the address and phone number of which I hadn't yet taken time to learn. So I just began pointing. "Over there. I live over there ... my family lives over there ... I live with them ... I mean we just moved in ... but I don't know the address ... or the phone number ... and no one's home."

That was all they needed to diagnosis that I was an idiot. They strapped me down to the spine board and rushed me to the emergency room, where I received a whopping two stitches to the back of my head.

While that was not one of my proudest moments in skateboarding, it does highlight a state that many of us spend most of our lives in—being so close to home and not knowing where it is. Being surrounded by God and still unaware of Him ... unable to recognize Him. How lonely and disorienting it can be in this life to crash and burn or hit a wall and not know where home is.

This is why we must start from where our bigger story begins. How can I ever expect to know myself and know God if I don't start with where and Whom I come from? With the One that I am OF?

I may not know you or your story, but I do know this about you: I know where your story begins. Before you ever knew His name, there was a God who knew yours. A God who loves you and whose image you were born to bear. A God in whose identity you share. *He* is the place to begin if you are ever going to understand *You*.

Of Community ...
for Community

The Creative Dance of the Trinity (Gen. 1:26)

The story of God actually begins *before* the beginning. In other words, there is a story deeper and older and far beyond our frail and finite human comprehension—a grand story that pre-existed our little story. It is a story that, unlike ours, has no beginning—a story that is more real than we can ever understand or imagine. But it is a story nonetheless.

It's the story of a God who already existed. A God who already existed in relationship, in community. A God who, in a way that only God could understand, has three unique dimensions that are all God but have a distinct identity within the Godhead. For hundreds of years, folks from theologians to Sunday school teachers have grasped at analogies to paint a simpler picture of the Trinity. But all the egg and ice-cube analogies in the world can't come close to describing the beauty and complexity of this relationship within God between the persons of the Trinity. It is far more relational than it is rational. This is why most metaphors fall short in attempting to explain the Trinity; the Trinity is not merely something to be explained rationally, but rather, something to be experienced relationally. As Stanley Grenz so brilliantly puts it,

> Because God himself is triune, we are in the image of God only as we enjoy community with others. Only as we live in fellowship can we show forth what God is like.
>
> Ultimately, then, the "image of God" is a social reality.[2]

---

2. Stanley Grenz, *Created for Community: Connecting Christian Belief with Christian Living*, 2nd ed. (Grand Rapids: Baker Academic, 2002), 80.

At the center of the Trinity we find relationship. A Divine, Loving, Giving, Eternal, Dynamic Relationship between God the Father, God the Son, and God the Holy Spirit. This is where you and I come from. All of us are *of* this *Us*. We are, as Grenz would say, created *from* community, *for* community. God created you to have relationship with Him and relationship with others. The relational implications of your "OFness" are epic. What if you actually *were* created for relationship? What if that were at the center of who you are? Not simply self-discovery, or self-advancement, or self-preservation … but relationship. Maybe this is why Jesus was able to sum up the entire Old Testament with bumper-sticker simplicity: "Love God with all of who you are. Love others more than you love yourself" (Luke 10:27 paraphrased). Be in loving relationship with God, and be in loving relationship with other people. If relationship is what you are created *from*, how could it not be what you are created *for*?

Think about it: No one had to teach you to make friends. You may have had to learn how to share or play nice, but your desire for relationship is hardwired into your DNA. No one had to convince you to fall in love, to give your heart to another. Regardless of the nature of your relationships, the desire for relationship is undeniable. Did you ever wonder where that came from?

The Greeks had a word for the kind of relational dynamic found in the Trinity. They called it *perichoresis*. It describes the fluid mutual indwelling and intersecting of the three persons of the Trinity. It's where we get our word *choreography*. That's how they described how the Trinity works—like a "Divine Dance." It is a dance that has been going on long before time. It's the dance that you came from and are invited into today.

Years ago, for Valentine's Day, I gave my wife, Jeanne, a set of Private Couples Dancing Lessons. Truth be told … the dance lessons were more for me than they were for Jeanne. The "private" part was to save her any additional embarrassment from having to dance with me. While I showed up ready to work on something more contemporary, say a couple's pop-and-lock breakdancing routine, our instructor had different plans. She took us back to the basics—the waltz, the cha-cha, and the fox trot (you know, the moves that all the cool kids are into these days).

Shortly into our first session, the dance instructor began to notice a pattern that is consistent for our dancing as well as our marriage. With forced patience, she observed, "You're both trying to lead. You both can't lead. One of you leads and the other follows. And in dances like these ... it's the *man* who leads."

"Finally!" I yelled out (perhaps too loud and too soon). So Jeanne obliged. I would be the leader. She would follow my direction. This lasted through roughly half of the next song, until Jeanne began to whisper in my ear, "Left, one two ... right, three four." She couldn't help herself. And apparently the dance instructor couldn't help us, because she quit after the next session.

This is not what we see in the *perichoresis* of the Trinity. Their dance is ever in sync because it is mutually submissive. The Father serves the Son, the Son serves the Spirit, the Spirit serves the Father. It is this dance that weaves its way throughout the pages of the Bible, throughout the very existence of our world, and through our very lives, starting in the very beginning.

In Genesis 1:26 we see it: "Then God said, 'Let *us* make human beings in *our* image, in *our* likeness ...'" (emphasis added).

There it is, written into the first few lines of our existence. We come from and belong to the beautiful dance of relationship that exists within the Trinity. So perfectly aligned and in sync that they move as one.

Father, Son, Holy Spirit.

Unique. Distinct. One.

This is what we see in the creation account. The dance of Father, Son, and Spirit is matched step-by-step through Adam and Eve. Like small children standing on their parents' feet to dance with them. It is most likely that Adam and Eve weren't even aware of how intuitive and effortless their relationship with God and each other truly was. But it was there, found in the unforced rhythms of grace that reverberated throughout the garden. This is what you were created for. Community is coded into the core of your DNA.

You are meant to join in the divine dance that you were created from and created for.

Each week I get a glimpse of how wonderful and how much work this can truly be. For the last couple of years I have had the privilege of leading a men's small group at Soul City. It has become one of the highlights of my week. I had never really been in a "men's group" for any significant amount of time before leading this one. And that absence wasn't by accident.

Somewhere in my subconscious I had formed a resistance to men's groups that stemmed from equal parts perception and experience. I had been a part of a couple of short-lived men's accountability groups that began with the greatest of intentions, but often ended up being nothing more than weekly "sin check-ins." Every one of those groups failed or fell apart after a couple months. So, to be honest, I wasn't sure what to expect when my friend Marc and I decided to lead a men's group together. All I knew is that I needed one. I needed a circle of relationships in which I could be myself. A circle of relationships that I could share my life with, not just the parts where I messed up, but all of it. I figured there might be others who needed the same. I simply had no idea how many that would end up being.

Our group started out with about ten guys. We met Friday mornings at 6:30. This time quickly became sacred and significant. We met at the church. I made the coffee. Each guy was tasked with bringing donuts for one week ... until one of them outdid us all by bringing a pan full of homemade French toast, egg casserole, and thick-cut bacon. We quickly voted him "Permanent Breakfast Bringer."

Sometimes we would read a book together or study aspects of the Bible. Sometimes we would stay in the big circle; other times we would break into smaller ones. We learned how to connect with one another without wasting time on small talk. We made an agreement that we would hold nothing back from one another. No truth, no encouragement, no challenge, no prayer, no tears — nothing would be held back. And if we sensed someone was holding back, we'd call him on it. Our little group grew from 10 to 16 to 20 to 36 guys in the course of a little over a year. It has since spawned off into several other men's groups that meet on various days each week in various places in the city.

All of this serves as evidence to me that what at first I most resisted was in truth what I most desired: the connection of community. The divine thread that I am woven from is what binds me to others. Your desire to connect runs deep, because it is one of the truest things about you. And it is some of the greatest evidence that you come from and belong to a relational God.

Better Questions = Better Answers

A little-known fact about me is that despite all the time I spend with people and in front of people, I am not actually the extrovert people assume I am. I am in fact a "Functional Introvert." I love people. I love having fun with people. I love making connections,... but I reenergize best when I'm by myself.

If there's a litmus test for whether you're an extrovert or introvert, it has to be "small talk." Small talk is a dividing line between extroverts and introverts. I love getting to know people, but I have an allergic reaction to small talk: I break out in "conversation" hives. Maybe it has something to do with the depth (or lack thereof) of the questions we ask in small talk. You know what they are,

> "How's it going?"
> "Where are you from?"
> "What do you do?"
> "Can you believe this snow/rain/heat/wind/construction we're having?" (I'm from Chicago, and this represents roughly 76 percent of what we talk about ... the rest is sports.)

Small-talk questions are fine and have their place—such as at your spouse's company Christmas party—but I think there are better questions. Questions that really matter. Questions that get to the core of who we are. Questions that reveal us and come to define us. In fact, there are two questions that every person throughout human history—regardless of cultural context, religious or nonreligious conviction—has had to face. While both questions are critical, it should be known that one actually comes before the other. Both are connected, but one is dependent on the other.

Those two questions are:

Who is God?

Who am I?

I believe that all of us, in our deepest thoughts and on our darkest nights, have wrestled with these two critical questions in one way or another.

While neither question can be fully answered this side of heaven, they must not be ignored. And not surprisingly, there are clues and cues as to their answers woven into the creation story ... right there in the beginning.

What does Genesis 1–2 reveal about who *God* is?

- God already exists in the context of community found in the Trinity.
- God creates out of overflowing love and delights in His Creation.
- God placed His Divinity into your Identity.
- It was God's will to give you Free Will—the choice to accept or reject Him.

And what does Genesis 1–2 reveal about who we are?

- You come from and belong to God.
- You are created for relationship with God and others.
- You are created to experience Equality in your relationships.
- You are meant to have Purpose in this life.

All of that is all there ... in the beginning.

And all of it points to the bigger truth that connects these two critical questions: You are OF God.

A God Who Speaks and Breathes (Genesis 1 – 2)

I find it interesting that some of the first things God does in the creation story and in our story are seemingly quite human. God speaks, and God breathes. God speaks our existence into existence. He speaks, and at the sound of His voice, galaxies form. Time as we know it is formed. Darkness and light are formed. Land, sea, and air are formed. Life is formed. *We* are formed. Before human language is ever formed, God speaks ... and humans are formed!

But God goes one step further. The writer of Genesis paints a picture of God leaning into His freshly spoken creation, scooping up a handful of red earth, and breathing His life into it. God creates something from His creation. In the same way He spoke the world into existence, He breathed humanity into existence. Nothing else in all of creation gets the breath of God. Everything came from His voice, but we are what came from His lungs. We don't just come from God; we come from deep inside God.

Life in a Garden
(Genesis 2)

A Little Bit of Nudity and Not an Ounce of Shame

As a kid I was always interested in the story of Adam and Eve. It had very little to do with the theological implications of creation, or original sin, or whether or not Adam and Eve got to ride dinosaurs in the garden of Eden. No. There was one single element to the story that I was most interested in—the fact that they were *naked*. They walked around, ate lunch, and gardened completely in the nude.

Genesis 2:25 says, "Now the man and his wife were both naked, but they felt no shame" (NLT).

Naked *but* no shame! That's the real miracle—no shame. No need to hide, cover, or conceal. No insecurity, no need for privacy, no big deal. Just naked ... and unashamed. How long has it been since you felt that way—totally exposed and totally safe? When was the last time you were emotionally, physically, relationally, or spiritually exposed, raw, real, honest, out there ... and unafraid? Not worried a single bit about how you would be perceived or thought of, or judged, or rejected? When was the last time you *really* shared what you were *really* feeling without hesitation or fear of misinterpretation? How long has it been since someone asked you, "How are you doing?" and you answered in a way that was actually consistent with how you were really doing? When was the last time you looked in the mirror and accepted your body for what it is and where it's at? When was the last time you wrenched your heart out before God, crying, screaming, kicking, or sitting in the stubborn resolve of silence?

Do we have any clue in our image-driven, self-protective, cynical, and ultimately insecure world what true nakedness must have been like? To be vulnerable, to be honest—while at the same time being totally unconditionally loved, safe, and secure.

Humanity lost more than a little skin in the garden. We lost vulnerability as the norm rather than the exception that it has become. We lost an eyes-wide-open wonder at the beauty of the body and replaced it with objectification and sexualization. We lost an openness and availability that our souls still hunger for. Thousands of years later, Jesus would redeem these things at their deepest levels through the cross and tomb. But two thousand years after the cross and the tomb, in a world marred and marked by sin, there is still a part of each of us wandering lost in that garden and searching for the renewal of all things. Searching for the innocence that was lost and will one day be made whole and new and better in the presence of God throughout eternity. One day, shame won't even be a part of our vocabulary.

Sowing Seeds of Equality

There is a seed planted in the garden that was all but uprooted once sin entered in. Yet it's there, planted deep in the soil of creation. It is the seed of *equality*. This seed grows out of the relationship between the Trinity that we are OF. Its fruit is a right and ripe way of relating to God and each other that we were all created for.

The Genesis 1 account of the Creation gives us a broad overview:

> So God created mankind in his own image,
> in the image of God he created them;
> male and female he created them.
> God blessed them and said to them, "Be fruitful and increase in number; fill the earth and subdue it. Rule over the fish in the sea and the birds in the sky and over every living creature that moves on the ground." (Gen. 1:27–28)

Notice how no special effort is given to highlight or underscore any form of hierarchy between Adam and Eve in Genesis 1. There is a hierarchy between humans and the earth. The command in Genesis 1:27 is to "subdue" the earth. The Hebrew word for "subdue" is *kavash*, which means to bring under control. So humans are to take care of the earth and not let it grow out of control.

There is also a hierarchy between humans and animals. Adam and Eve are commanded to "rule over" fish and birds and all other animals. The Hebrew word here is *radah*. Its meaning is most closely associated with the idea of ruling by going down, wandering about, and being among. All of this leadership that Adam and Eve are commanded to do is loving leadership. God commanded "them" to *kavash* and *radah*. God commanded Adam *and* Eve to rule over together. The command is mutual, and the work is to be shared equally.

When we get to Genesis 2, we get a little greater detail. Shortly after creation, God puts Adam to work in the garden. And it's not long after that that God acknowledges his deep and divine need for community.

> The LORD God said, "It is not good for the man to be alone. I will make a helper suitable for him" (v. 18). So God created Eve.

Now, it would be easy to assume here that we have our first introduction to hierarchy in the story based on a couple of assumptions.

First is the whole idea of *Order*. The idea is that Adam came before Eve, so he must be "over" her. But if order determined authority, then humans would actually be ruled by dogs and cats and woodchucks. While that makes for great Sci-Fi, that's not how it works in the real world. So order can't determine authority.

Then there's the word *Helper*. God said that He would make Adam a suitable "helper." The assumption might be that Eve's job is to "help" Adam accomplish all the work that God had for him. Kind of like a teacher's aid or a superhero sidekick. But that's not actually what the word "helper" means in Genesis 2.

The original Hebrew word for "helper" is *'ezer*. According to R. David Freedman, the word *'ezer* is a combination of two roots, meaning "to rescue, to save" and "strength."[3] The word appears 21 times throughout the Old Testament. It appears twice in reference to Eve, three times in reference to a military context, and 16 times

---

3. R. David Freedman, "Woman, a Power Equal to a Man," in *Biblical Archaeology Review* 9 (1983), 56.

in reference to God. God is our rescuer, our strength, the One who saves. Not the God who is our sidekick, or the God who is our assistant, but the God who saves—our 'Ezer. This is how God decides to introduce us to Eve. She is a partner to Adam who rescues and saves him from isolation and helps him accomplish and enjoy all that God has given them to do. She is his equal, and together they set out to enjoy the beauty of community in the context of equality.

Equality is essential to biblical community. Equality is not the absence of distinction, but rather the celebration of it. The Father is distinct from the Son, but celebrates the Son. The Son is distinct from the Spirit, but celebrates the Spirit. The Man is distinct from the Woman, but celebrates her. The Woman is distinct from the Man, but celebrates him. It's a posture that was broken by sin and is sorely missed in our world today. But it is something that, for a season, *thrived* in the garden—a direct reflection of the Trinity that we are created of and the life we are created for.

The Purpose of Purpose

As we dig deeper into the first two chapters of the Bible, we not only discover the absence of shame and the presence of equality, but also find something else at work: *purpose.* In Genesis 2, God gives us a glimpse into who He is and who we are meant to be by including one often overlooked detail in Adam's short-lived residency in the garden. Genesis 2:15, 19–20 point out that

> The LORD God took the man and put him in the Garden of Eden to work it and take care of it....
>
> Now the LORD God had formed out of the ground all the wild animals and all the birds in the sky. He brought them to the man to see what he would name them; and whatever the man called each living creature, that was its name. So the man gave names to all the livestock, the birds in the sky and all the wild animals.

Shortly after God rested from the work of Creation, He put Adam to work. God immediately gave Adam purpose: not just something to do, but something to give himself to.

God: "Adam, I have a job for you. It's called 'gardening.'"
Adam: "What's a garden?"
God: "You're living in one."
Adam: "Right ... what's gardening?"
God: "It's taking care of where you live. I make it; you take care of it. Sound good?"
Adam: "Sure. Anything else?"
God: "Actually, yes. When you're done gardening, I'm going to need you to do a little sorting and labeling ... of every species of every animal in the world."

Adam was not only the first human being, but also the first employee. God didn't have to give Adam anything to do. I mean, the guy was just a pile of dirt a couple days before. Let's take this one step at a time ... literally: Adam should learn how to walk before he rakes, but instead God gives Adam purpose. God invites Adam to participate in creation, to work with Him in the care of the earth. And then there's the naming of the animals. Best job ever!

God: "Adam, what about this one? It's got a long tail and loves to run fast."
Adam: "A horse?"
God: "Good. How about this one? It's white, loves to fly, a real peaceful thing."
Adam: "A glove? No, wait ... dove!"
God: "I like it. How about this one? I'll be honest—it's not my best work. It's temperamental, self-absorbed, hard to handle. And honestly, kind of annoying."
Adam: "A cat?"
God: "Perfect!"

Adam had purpose. He worked. But more than that, he worked with God. He worked in partnership with his Creator in creation—because God is a God at work, as we see in the creation account earlier in Genesis 2:

By the seventh day God had finished the work he had been doing; so on the seventh day he rested from all his work. Then God blessed the seventh day and made it holy, because on it he rested from all the work of creating that he had done. (vv. 2–3)

God is teaching us that there is work to be done, and when it's done, there is rest to be had. And the truth about God is that He continues to work to this very day. He has yet to start pulling from His retirement. He wasn't just contracted out for creation; He is still at work today. God was at work this morning when the sun rose and this evening when it set. God is at work as the seasons change. God is at work when snow falls in the Midwest—and then keeps falling—and then doesn't go away for six months. God is still at work in our tiny little planet, and He is still at work in sustaining the entire universe. God is a God who works. He is a God who takes great pleasure and has great purpose in His work ... and you and I are created to join in with Him.

You and I were created by God to work. But more than that, we were created by God to enjoy our work by working *with* Him. That's what gives work purpose—when I work *with* and *for* God, regardless of what it is. Whatever it is that you do, you can do it with the God who created you and created you to do it! Adam worked because God works. We work because it's a part of who we are OF. Your life is meant to have purpose. And in God it actually does.

A Short-Lived Shalom

In this first movement of the story of the Bible, OF, all was well. All was as it should be. There was presence and purpose and equality and vulnerability. This first season of creation was perfection. And that perfection was merely a small reflection of the far greater reality of a perfect God.

When I was in high school, I visited Disney World in Orlando, Florida, for the very first time. As a kid growing up on the West Coast, I knew Disneyland like the back of my hand, but Disney World was so new ... so vast ... so expansive ... and so expensive.

We spent a day at Epcot with its geodesic dome, its World of Motion, and its lack of any exciting rides or anything that a teenager would be remotely interested in.

There was, however, one thing that was interesting: the World Showcase. It is the half of the park that is dedicated to replicating eleven different countries from around the world — from the architecture, to the food, to the people they cast to walk around and work the attractions. It's all pretty amazing. Have you ever wanted to eat "authentic" sushi while shopping for wooden clogs and while listening to African tribal music? You can do it at Epcot! It was all there. Smaller than real life, but bigger than anything I'd ever seen or experienced. All of it so carefully replicated to give me the experience of being somewhere I'd never been before.

It didn't matter that what I was experiencing wasn't truly authentic, but rather an artificial replication based on stereotypical constructs, because the girls working the Norway exhibition were all I wanted to see. They were absolutely beautiful! They were the reason I suddenly became interested in the world. My brother Justin and I rode the Maelstrom (the ride in the Norway exhibition) a solid seven times. We rode it so many times that we actually walked out speaking Norwegian. (In retrospect, it never once dawned on us that these beautiful "Norwegian" girls weren't actually from Norway at all, but most likely part-time students at Valencia Community College. The illusion worked. Well played, Mr. Disney!)

The garden of Eden is a lot like Epcot (minus the outrageous price of admission). It is a small representation of a much bigger thing. It is what heaven would look like on earth. It is the physical form of a spiritual realm, a glimpse of that world in this world. In it, as in heaven, God's presence exists, and thus with it comes the full Shalom of God. *Shalom* is an ancient Hebrew word that in its simplest understanding means "peace." But that word, like a gem, can be turned again and again to reveal a much bigger and beautiful picture. Shalom encompasses peace, contentment, completeness, and the overwhelming sense that all is well. Shalom is the atmosphere of heaven, and the garden of Eden was our glimpse of that here on earth. Jeff Van Duzer,

Dean of Seattle Pacific University, writes, "The Garden was filled with a rich, satisfying and balanced peace—Shalom."[4]

And that's exactly what it was—Shalom. From working with God to care for creation, to the creation of Eve and the introduction of intimacy, to walks with God in the cool of the day, there was in the garden an undeniable peace. Shalom was to be the context for our existence, the soil in which our relationship with God would grow. It would be as close as we would get to heaven on earth ... for a time.

Can you imagine a world existing in and defined by the Shalom of God? The overwhelming sense that all is well. No fear. No anxiety. No loneliness. No poverty. No sin. Nothing separating you from the power and presence of God. The thought of it causes a small ache in the deepest reaches of the soul, like feeling homesick for a place you've never known. A longing for a place you've never been. This is the ache of eternity planted within you (see Ecclesiastes 3:11). An ever-present albeit elusive sense that, while you are fully at home, this world is not fully what it was intended to be. A sense that there was a time when the Shalom of God was as real as the air we breathed, that it was not contained by the confines of heaven, but that it defined everything contained in this world. That heaven had a zipcode.

That's what it means to be OF God—you were made by Him, in His image, to live in His world surrounded by His love. And even though it was short-lived in this chapter of our story, this is not the end of the story. There is a time coming when the Shalom of God will once again define heaven and earth. The line between the two shall be erased. And what was meant to be will finally be forevermore.

Hand in Hand with God

Living in the city, as my family does, means that greenery is at a premium. We are surrounded by grey. So every park or patch of grass becomes a sacred space. The townhome we are living in while I write this doesn't have a yard. This is a first for us. Our home in

---

4. Jeff Van Duzer, *Why Business Matters to God: And What Still Needs to Be Fixed* (Downers Grove, IL: IVP Academic, 2010), 210.

Atlanta had three-fourths of an acre of land. We don't even have three-fourths of an inch of grass here. We do, however, have planters full of plants—seventeen planters, to be exact. And by "we" I mean Jeanne. She loves her plants, herbs, succulents, and flowers. She breathes their fragrance and aroma not simply into her lungs, but also into her soul. And she takes care of them. Carefully planting them at the right time, in the right place, learning what does well where and when. And she waters them, prunes them, and does just about whatever they need—with the exception of talking to them. It takes work. It takes time. But it gives life to her and is a gift to our family and to anyone who visits us.

Our growth with God is not all that different. No one ever drifts into the life they were created to live. There are always intentional choices and steps that go into your growth. It never happens on its own. When it comes to becoming who God created you to be, it never happens by yourself. God is always the One who ultimately grows you. But that doesn't mean that you don't have a part to play. When it comes to your growth, there are things that only *God* can do … and things that only *you* can do.

Creating you—*only God*. Empowering you with the Holy Spirit—*only God*. Giving you spiritual gifts—*only God*. Forgiving you when you sin and make a mess of your life—*only God*. There are many things about your spiritual growth that only *God* can do, but similarly, there are some things that *only you* can do. Saying "yes" to God's offer of love and life—*only you*. Showing up with your personal spiritual practices—*only you*. Surrounding yourself with people who are going to help you grow—*only you*.

For reasons known only to God, He decides to partner with you in your growth … hand in hand—just as He did with Adam and Eve in the garden. You are invited to cultivate the soil of your soul together with God. It is a beautiful collision of omnipotence and ownership. God has all the power to simply make you into what you are meant to be, but He chooses to intentionally leave a gap between His will and your willingness. That gap is called growth. And you have a part to play in it!

Remember that in the beauty and glory of creation, God still put Adam to work. God left room in His perfection for partnership. Adam was invited to partner with God in the cultivation of creation. And you are invited to nothing less. God has planted a seed of His glory and identity in you. Buried deep in the soil of your life is the life God has for you. There, beneath the circumstances and story of your life, is the You whom God desires you to be. He has already done everything that needed to be done *for* you, and now He is ready and waits to work *with* you in the story and glory of your growth. Will you join Him? Will you choose to align your life with the life that God has for you? Will you do what *only you* can do to become who *only God* can help you become? Will you live and lean into the One that you are OF?

10 Percent You

Recently our third grader, Elijah, came home from school having just had his mind blown.

"Dad!" he started. "Did you know that human beings only use ten percent of their brains?!? It's true. Just ten percent! And did you know that if we were able to use one hundred percent of our brains, we could do all kinds of things?"

"Really?" I asked, rather intrigued. "Like what?"

"Like fly ... and time travel ... and lift things with our minds. We wouldn't *ever* have to go to school, 'cause we'd know *everything*!"

"That's sounds *awesome*, son!" I replied. "Where'd you learn this? One of your teachers?"

Elijah responded without missing a beat, "No! Teachers aren't gonna tell you this kinda stuff! I learned it from Henry ... and Henry knows a *lot*, Dad!"

Actually, despite as much as Henry knows, he isn't the first person to share this "discovery." There is an urban myth out there that I'm sure you've heard or maybe have even shared. It basically states that the average human only uses around 10 percent of their brain. While there's no way to scientifically prove that humans only use 10 percent, it's safe to say that large percentages of people are actually operating on significantly less that that ... and neuroscientists call them "men."

If the 10 Percent Brain Theory actually *were* true, it leads me to wonder: What's the other 90 percent doing? Where is it when I need it? I can think of several moves when Jeanne insisted that we bring the claw-foot tub (that she swore she was going to restore) with us ... a little mental levitation could have come in handy. The idea of 90 percent of our brain going unused is interesting to consider ... if only it were true. Unfortunately, despite what Henry says, it is not.

But building on that same assumption, I would like to propose another "discovery." Through all the years I have spent with spiritual directors, mentors, and counselors through all the counseling and conversations I have had with others, I have come to believe that the average human is operating on about 10 percent of their True Identity. I believe that at our best, we are hovering somewhere around 10 percent of whom we were actually created by God to be. That while we were each created to be a glimpse of God in this world, bearing likeness to who we are OF, most of us only ever get a glimpse of who we truly are.

Imagine taking a road trip with only 10 percent of the directions you needed to get there. Think you might get lost? Or imagine making a brand-new meal with only 10 percent of the recipe. The results would be interesting, to say the least. It is no different with your God-given identity. The less you know about your God-given identity, who you are OF, the further and further you drift. The more lost you will become in this life. The less you will live the life God that desires for you.

Can you imagine what it would look like for you to be operating out of even 10 percent *more* of the truth of whom God created you to be? What might be different in your marriage if you were 20 percent more of whom God created you to be rather than whom you've become? How would you approach your work differently if you had 50 percent greater understanding of whom God has created you to be? Would you continue to work how you've been working? Would you continue to work *where* you've been working? Would your friends or family even recognize you? Would you recognize yourself?

You see, the real myth is not just that you are operating out of 10 percent of your God-given identity, but rather, that this is as good as it gets. The myth you may believe goes something like, "This is just who I am. It's how I've always been. It's how I'll always be." If this myth is true, then grace and growth might as well be a myth too. If all you ever are is who you are now, then redemption is nothing more than a one-time event, and transformation is but a pipe dream. If you "are who you are," then God is no longer all that necessary as the Author and Perfecter of your life and faith and will most likely be reassigned to a middle management position in the department of Crisis Management.

This is the way many folks go about life, but this is no way to live. You were created by God for more. And it should come as a great relief and no great surprise that the single greatest way for you to become more *you* is for you to be more with God. The more you are with God, the more you become yourself. The more you live your one and only life with God, the more you discover that transformation is not only possible … it's expected.

I think of a woman from our church named Erin. She has spent the better part of her adult life in broken relationship with her family. The details of how their family bond broke down are complex and compounded by time. Needless to say, Erin had come to believe that this was just how it was going to be for her and her family—that "broken" was the new norm. But I've watched over the past few years as Erin has opened her life up more and more to God, how she has let hope heal her hard heart, and how God is lovingly leading her to the part that she has played in her family dynamics. I've watched God take things from "as good as it gets" to "better than I ever imagined"—to the point that this past Thanksgiving, after more than a decade, Erin's family sat down around the table together.

I have watched it in my friend Jason's life. Growing up African American in a largely white area of Texas, Jason had assumed that the racial differences that often divide were set in stone. Even in church ... sometimes *especially* in church. He assumed that this is just how it is, and there's nothing that any of us can really do about it. But over the past three years I've seen Jason grow significantly in his relationship with God. I've seen God move him from "indifference" to "difference maker"! The more Jason sought the God of justice and equality, the more he began to see how he was created in God's image.

So, prompted by God, Jason moved out of his downtown Chicago loft and into Lawndale (one of Chicago's poorest and roughest neighborhoods). Jason is forming a theology of equality, and instead of giving up on the church, he has dug in and has become in our church one of the leading voices for racial equality.

I have seen this kind of transformation in my own life. I grew up in a loving home and a great church, but I still managed to pick up along the way that lie that I am not "enough." It's the lie at the root of shame. Despite incredible blessings, opportunities, and even success, I still believed that I wasn't worthy of any of it and that it was only a matter of time until everyone else figured out what I already knew. This was my secret story—one that I not only believed to be true, but thought would never change.

However, this is not the story that God has for my life, because this is not the story of Genesis 1–2. The story found there is of a God who pours out His love and blessing because He is good and makes all who receive it worthy in the process. The more I began to get to know the God who calls me His "beloved," the more I began to see how loved I am and who I really am in light of that love. Over the last several years I have seen God help me uproot the lie of shame in my life. In its uprooting I am seeing, like never before, the fruit of gratitude, the presence, and the richness of living out of the truth of who I really am in God.

This is what happens when we bring even 10 percent of our true selves to God. The truth of the creation story found in Genesis 1–2 can change your story. When you know this, God leads to knowing who you truly are. As John Calvin said, "There is no knowing that does not begin with knowing God."

The End of the Beginning (Genesis 3)

Every beginning has an ending. Every job, every relationship, every season eventually comes to an end. Despite any of our delusional denial of this reality, we all, at some level, know that this is true. Just think about some of the endings that you've already experienced in your life. Some were welcomed—graduation, puberty, a difficult season. Some endings were not welcomed—a divorce, losing a job, the death of someone you love. There are endings that we plan for and endings that surprise us. But it is inevitable that every beginning has an ending. The same is true of the first movement of the Bible. Eden has an ending.

The beautiful beginning of our story was ultimately shattered by sin. That space between God's will and our willingness is often referred to by theologians and philosophers as "free will." We tend to think of it as "choice." God deliberately created us with the ability to choose Him ... or reject Him. It was a space that was intended for our growth, but was ultimately sabotaged and substituted with sin. Humanity made their choice ... and it wasn't God.

When Adam and Eve chose to eat of the fruit from the Tree of the Knowledge of Good and Evil (Gen. 3:1–7), they brought an ending to the beginning. The beginning of sin was the end of the garden of Eden. That single ending would usher in the beginning of the longest section in the story of the Bible. For tens of thousands of years, sin would stand *between* us and God. And God would continue to be *between* us and the consequences of our sin. This is where the story of God is heading at the end of Genesis 2 ... but that doesn't diminish the significance of where our story starts.

Even though the first movement in the story of God (OF) is by far the shortest, that doesn't make it any less important. Remember, our story started in glory. All was as it was meant to be. The beginning was good. But as we are going to see over the next chapter, it would not stay that way for long. It all went terribly wrong. Shalom was shattered. Perfection was poisoned. Paradise was paralyzed. And our relationship with God and one another was in ruins. All of this comes out of and after OF, and in some ways continues to this day. We are still living with the fallout of the Fall.

But as we will see throughout the story of the Bible and the course of this book, sin is not the end of the story. All was not lost at the end of the beginning. That is because planted in the sin-soaked soil at the end of Eden was a seed of salvation. The seed was One who would not only restore things to the way they were, but actually redeem all things in such a way as to give meaning to it all.

In Genesis 3:15, as God is rolling out the repercussions of sin, He gives a glimpse into a redemptive future and the cost that it would come by. He says to Satan,

> "I will put enmity [division] between you and the woman, and between your offspring [the forces that oppose God] and hers [Jesus]; he will crush your head [definitive defeat], and you will strike his heel [death at the cross]."

This is the first recorded prophecy in the Bible, spoken from the very mouth of God. In other words, what God is saying is that while sin brought an ending, Jesus brings a new beginning.

This is what is going on behind the scenes of every page of the Old Testament. Every chapter becomes a countdown to the eventual rescue and redemption of all things lost in the garden.

It Started in a Garden for a Reason

It is my sneaking suspicion that God has a thing for gardens. The story of humanity begins in a garden. Jesus taught about our life and relationship with God using the metaphors of seeds, harvests, vineyards, branches, vines, and fruit. It was in a garden that Jesus prayed and pleaded and ultimately trusted and obeyed God just hours before the cross. Jesus was even buried in a garden tomb.

Isn't it interesting that sin enters into a garden and is ultimately defeated in a garden? I think God does some of His best work in gardens. But more than that, I know that God has a thing for growth. The point of a garden is to enjoy the beauty of something doing what it was meant to do: *grow!*

Years ago, I faced one of many invitations from God to join him in the garden of growth. I was not excited. I had spent most of my life avoiding any of the real pain that comes from transformation. I had worked hard to avoid the hard work of growth. But what had "worked" for most of my life wasn't working any more. Up to that point, my relationship with God had been built on a premise (that I assumed was reality) that as long as I was good to God, He would be good to me. In other words, "God, I'll follow You, make good choices, try and avoid bad ones, so long as You are good to me and keep pain and loss as far away from my life as possible." Sounds like a good deal, right? Unfortunately, as I look back on that mental contract now, I can't seem to find God's signature anywhere on it. God loves me too much to let me stay stuck.

The cracks in the foundation of the relationship I had built with God were not only starting to show, but were starting to grow. I was having a crisis of faith. I was in the middle of writing a book about God, and the truth is, I had never felt farther from Him. My job was changing greatly. And on top of that we suffered the sudden and shocking loss of Jeanne's dad, Bill. It was not any one of these things on its own per se, but the slow and rising tide of it all that led me to the point of a decision: Am I going to go around this difficult season of life or am I going to grow through it? Do I want the life that God has for me on the other side to walk through this season of growth?

Round about this time, my spiritual director gave me a metaphor that has held true almost a decade later. She said that there are times when God flies us over the desert and lovingly kicks us out of the plane for our own good. In other words, some of us are so stubborn or love control so much that God lovingly allows circumstances in our lives that loosen our supposed grip, awaken our awareness and dependence on Him, and cause us to grow like never before. "This,

however, is not what God is doing with you," she said. "God is inviting you into the desert that comes before growth. You must choose
this winter, if you are ever going to have spring. God is inviting you
to put on a backpack, walk to the end of the cul de sac of comfort,
and step into the desert that is in front of you. Will you get by, or will
you grow through? Your next season of growth is contingent on your
choice. You must choose."

If I was going to grow, I would have to put one foot in front of
the other and walk into the desert of broken idols. The place where
people go to let go of their false gods. The desert filled with the sand
on which I had built my house. The desert where the Israelites spent
forty years wandering. The desert that runs through the valley of the
shadow of death. The desert that Jesus journeyed through when He
was tempted, tested, and tried by Satan. The desert of dark nights of
the soul. The desert that ultimately leads to a garden.

This was my choice. Would I do what was needed to become
whom God intended? Did I think I could get to spring without
going through fall and winter? Would I grow, or would I stay stuck?
Ultimately, I decided that the pain of growth was better to face than
the numbness of stagnancy. Per God's invitation, I walked into that
desert ... kicking and screaming, but I walked nonetheless. I spent
about two years there. Two years of weekly morning meetings with
my spiritual director. Two years of counseling (which has turned into
twelve ... and counting). Two years of preaching about God on the
weekends and wrestling with Him throughout the week. Two years
of unpacking a god that I had created over the previous twenty years
of my life. Two years of regularly choosing to walk through the valley
of the shadow of death that leads to life. Two years that were utterly
essential to my having a real relationship with the God Who created
me and apparently ... wasn't done with me.

I would love to tell you that that was my last trip there. It was not.
God continues to send me invitations to walk the high and narrow
path that winds its way through the desert, but leads to growth and
life. My treks through the desert have become more frequent in the
past few years. Time in the desert has become a part of the rhythm of

my growth. I continue to find more and more things in me that need
to die, so that God can grow me more and more into who I actually
am in Him. It's never fun. It's never easy. I never go looking for it.
But I'm always grateful for it on the other side. I'm learning that life
with God is a life of growth. That there is no growth without a little
death. That there is no garden without a desert. That there is no new
beginning without an old thing ending. And that stepping into the
life God has for me means learning how to walk with a little sand
in my shoes.

Conclusion: From OF to BETWEEN

When I consider those early days in Eden, I am struck by how
God knew all along that the unique season of OF would only be just
that—a season. Our all-knowing God knew all along that those
days in paradise were numbered. He knew which walk through the
garden together with Adam and Eve in the cool of the day would
be their last. He had to have known at the time He saw them laugh
with a joy, absent from the deep pain that would come with sin, that
it would be the last. He knew which night would be the last night
that they would sleep under the trees he planted for them, naked,
present, fearing nothing. He had to have known that Lucifer, that
fallen angel, would not stay down, but forcibly enter himself into the
story in an attempt to destroy what God loves.

I wonder, at the moment sin entered in, if God felt the phantom
pain that would come one day from having to turn His back on His
own Son when the totality of sin was poured out upon Him. While
you and I will never know what God knows, I believe He knew
all along. I believe He knew it all and all that was to come ... and
still loved. He was still present. And despite the choice of sin and
the rejection of Him that was to come ... there was no preemptive
turning of God's back.

The same is true of our relationship with God today. God created
you. He created you with that same intentional space between His
will and your willingness. He is in no way surprised by your sin. And

He's not surprised by mine. He does not turn His back from me, even though I regularly and repeatedly turn my back on Him. This is Good News—better news than we even realize.

Before moving on to the next chapter, take a moment to reflect on how significantly the story is about to change. Reflect on how sin changed our world, our relationship with each other, and our relationship with God. Everything changed the moment sin entered in. This is the moment right before that reality. This is the blank page the next chapter. This is the last inhale of the presence of perfection, just before the exhale of separation. This is the calm before the storm. This is the end of Eden and the beginning of BETWEEN.

4

Part Three

BETWEEN

Genesis 3 to Malachi 4

The Big Idea of the Small Word: BETWEEN

The second small word in the big story of God is the word BETWEEN. It represents the majority of the Old Testament. It's the time between when Sin entered in (Gen. 3) and when Grace entered in (the Gospels). The time between separation and restoration. The time between the First Adam and the new Adam (Rom. 5:12–18). The time between.

The word BETWEEN also encompasses what sin did when it entered our story: It came between God and us. It stood between us and each other. In the beginning, there was nothing in-between anything that mattered … now there was something that stood between everything that mattered most. The story of the Old Testament is about the time between and the length that God goes to come between us and the consequences of our sin.

Between. Satan first uttered the idea into existence. He convinced Adam and Eve that a tree stood *between* them and God's best. Immediately upon their taking a bite of that tree's fruit, it turned out that it was not a tree at all that stood between Adam and Eve and God, but rather sin. Sin worked its way between us and God.

When all was OF, there was no separation, no division, nothing between. There was perfect unity. But sin by its very nature brings with it separation. What once was one became divided. Sin separates not with a single solitary line, but by a million degrees of separation. Sin separates with an intensity matched only by the level of intimacy that was previously experienced in the garden. In other words, we have no idea how far we've fallen until we see just how close we once were. The reality of what life is like *outside* the garden is only given context by what life was like *in* the garden ... before sin came between.

In the previous chapter we explored just how beautiful, intimate, and effortless life was for all parties involved (Adam, Eve, the Trinity, heaven, earth, plants, and animals). Now we will explore something entirely different. Everything that was once effortless and intuitive became work and struggle in the days of between. The first-person access to God in the garden was replaced by a series of substitutions. Bridges between, built by God, that served as reminders that things are not as they once were ... or how they are supposed to be.

As you will see, the second movement in the story of God is easily the longest.

There is a great amount of territory to cover in this chapter. To sum up the totality of sin run amuck in the world over the course of thousands of years is no small task. But we can begin to understand this movement in the story of the Bible and this small word better by exploring the *impact* of sin. When we understand its roots and see the ramifications of how it comes between us and God throughout the course of the Old Testament, we begin to understand what BETWEEN really means.

The movement of the Old Testament tells story after story of In-Betweens. It's the story of a people on the move but never quite coming home. It's the story of how people respond to a God who is ever present but suddenly seemingly distant. It's the story of a God who continues to build bridges while His people continue to build walls. The story of a God who goes between through covenants, commandments, temples, priests, kings, and prophets.

In this chapter we will explore the Covenants Commitments of God found in the Old Testament. These covenant commitments are one of the first ways that God goes between us and the separation suffered by sin. They are one of the ways that God substituted His former presence with future promises. They are invitations to His people to trust His goodness, based on the evidence of His faithfulness ... even in the face of their unfaithfulness.

We will also explore the Commandments—the Law given to Moses to guide our everyday lives and our life with God. What Adam and Eve heard with their ears, generations would have to read with their eyes.

We will consider the temple and its priests. The temple is yet another way in the Old Testament by which God goes between by creating the first physical space since Eden where He promised His presence. The priests were the means by which the heart of God, which had largely been silent, would be given voice again.

Then we will look at and listen to the Psalms through the perspective of BETWEEN. They stand as the soul of the Old Testament—the feeling of *between* captured in gut wrenchingly honest prayer, poems, and praise.

Finally, we will look at the kings and subsequent prophets found in the Old Testament. The Israelites' demand for a king was a desire for something to go *between*. Like so many other examples in the Old Testament, the people worshiped the thing in-between rather than the God at the other end. And after the aftermath of the royal failure of the kings, God would speak to His people through His prophets—His final go-between in the Old Testament.

While the Old Testament can seem long, confusing, and intimidating, it is really just a story of In-Betweens. Every page paints a picture of what life is like at a "distance" from God and the lengths that God goes to build bridges between His people and our sin. The Old Testament consistently and convincingly shows us what life is like when we bring sin between us and God while at the same time demonstrating what God did, does, and will do by bringing a way between us and our sin.

The Cycle of Sin

When I was a kid, one of my best buddies was a guy named Demas Lamas III. You're not simply "given" a name like Demas Lamas III … you're *blessed* with it! Demas lived about a mile from my house, so we would spend our summers riding our bikes to each other's homes and then riding our bikes somewhere else together. One of our favorite places to go was Lake Elizabeth (a park, lake, and playground), in Fremont, California. Lake Elizabeth was about 2.5 miles from either of our houses. So, for those of you keeping score, that's 1 mile to either house, 2.5 miles to Lake Elizabeth, 2.5 miles back, and 1 mile home. That's 7 miles! And we were nine years old ... and we did it all the time ... on BMX bikes that weighed approximately 372 pounds!

Demas and I loved Lake Elizabeth, mostly for its "natural" lagoon. By "natural," I mean something that the city dug out and filled in with sand and water and then charged two dollars per visitor to enjoy—you know, natural. We would spend hours hanging out and swimming there. One particular visit stands out in my mind. We were getting ready to leave the lagoon and ride our bikes home. Our towels were twenty or so yards from the water, so as we walked back to the towels, our feet picked up a good bit of sand along the way.

We got to our towels, and out of frustration, Demas grunted, "Ughh! My feet are all sandy, I'm gonna go wash 'em off and then we can go. Be right back!" He proceeded to run back to the water, dip his feet in, wash them off, and walk back. Right when he arrived back to the towels, he grunted, "Doggone it! My feet are all sandy again! Hold on! I'm gonna go wash them off again." He retraced his steps down to the water, dipped his feet in, washed them off, and walked back.

Demas, not too surprisingly, looked down at his feet and this time didn't say anything. He didn't need to. He knew that his current strategy wasn't working. So he mentally regrouped, and after walking back to the water and washing off, he decided to run back. He ran as fast as he could, only to arrive at the same place ... again. This might have gone all day had not someone suggested that we wait until we're out of the sand and use our towels to wipe our feet off. The idea was so crazy that we thought it might just work. It did! Within minutes we were back on our bikes—feet clean, towels sandy, ready for the 2.5-mile ride home.

The story of the people of the Old Testament plays out much like the exploits of Demas and me at the beach. Once sin comes between us and God, as described in Genesis 3, it begins a cycle of sin that continues right up to the arrival of Jesus. The Old Testament is like a broken record, stuck in a pattern of a people close to God, then far from God, then coming back to God, then walking away from God, then crawling back, then running away.

The Old Testament is about remembering and forgetting and remembering and forgetting. It is such a back-and-forth relationship with God that you can put your finger in nearly any section in the Old Testament and find the people either walking with God or walking away from Him.

Like a giant spring turned on its side, there are times when the people of God are seemingly moving "up" and closer to Him. But those seasons are inevitably followed by periods of great decline and demise. And it is typically at the very bottom that the people of God finally give Him their attention and start coming back to Him ... only to eventually look down and see the sand still on their feet and begin the process all over again.

Maybe you can relate. If you have been in a relationship with God more than a little while, you have probably seen this pattern play out in your own life. I think of a friend of mine whom I met with a year ago at a very low point in his life and faith. His exterior world was falling apart around him, which had significant collateral damage on his interior world. He shared—in a sort of monotone voice with eyes that seemed like there were no more tears left—how far and distant he felt from God. In his words, "There's just nothing there." He had once been a leader in our church. He had helped several of his friends begin a relationship with Jesus, had led several small groups, and was sought after as a spiritual leader in our community. But in that moment ... there was just nothing there. He honestly wondered if he would ever feel close to God again ... and if he even wanted to.

Just recently I bumped into him—and there was something quietly different about him. There was peace in his eyes and joy in his voice. He shared how he, at his lowest, had been lovingly drawn back to God. Drawn to, in his words, "even deeper places" with God.

He had never felt closer—which is what I'm sure he would have said several years ago, before he had never felt further from God.

Maybe you have a similar story or have faced similar seasons in your life with God. These are the stories found in the Old Testament. Your story demonstrates in living color that your life with God is not an "up and to the right" kind of thing. It is a lot of ups and downs and a lot of time in-between.

Our story often mirrors the story and the cycle of the Old Testament. New characters, new contexts, new sins … same cycle. God extends Himself to His people. His people respond. All is well. God's people desire something other than God. God's people reject Him. God allows them to live in the consequences of their sin. God's people are broken and cry out to Him. God extends Himself to His people, and they respond. All is well. God's people desire something other than God and may reject Him. God allows them to live in the consequences of their sin. God's people are broken and cry out to Him. God extends Himself to His people. The cycle continues.

The Story Before the Story

A Rebellion in Heaven (Sometime Before Genesis 1)

While we typically tend to think of sin as something that first appears in the garden of Eden between God, Adam, and Eve, this is not actually where it begins. What we see in the garden are the first fruits of sin, but its roots go much, much deeper.

Our first glimpse of sin comes before our story even begins. It was wrapped in a revolt in heaven—a coup d'état aimed directly at God Himself. It was a revolution of betrayal fueled by pride and a fundamental misunderstanding of the heart and rule of God.

The details are not fully addressed in the Bible, and even if they were, I doubt that we could fully understand the depth of their meaning. But what we do know is that angels are somehow a part of the story. While no one is exactly clear when they were created, we know that they were created by the Trinity to be perfect and with a free will … just like you and me.

Among that heavenly multitude stood one of the most beautiful of all the angels—Lucifer. To this day that name slithers off our tongues with a sound of disdain as though it were whispered by a snake itself. But that is not how it was uttered originally in heaven. The name "Lucifer" means Bright One, Shining One, Brilliant One, and Morning Star. It was given to the most beautiful and one of the highest-ranking angels throughout all of heaven. Lucifer was beloved by God and held a special place of authority and adoration. But somehow, for Lucifer, that was not enough. As one assigned to bring worship to God, Lucifer determined and demanded that God should worship *him!* When God did not, he set out to lead a rebellion against God in heaven.

Passages such as Isaiah 14:12–14, Ezekiel 28, and Revelation 12:7–9 tell us that Lucifer attempted to violently overtake God's throne in heaven. The intensity and arrogance of his battle cry is found in Isaiah 14:13–14:

> "I will ascend to the heavens;
>> I will raise my throne above the stars of God;
> I will sit enthroned on the mount of assembly,
>> on the utmost heights of Mount Zaphon.
> I will ascend above the tops of the clouds;
>> I will make myself like the Most High."

While we don't know the details of that celestial battle, we do know that Satan was soundly defeated by God and was cast out of heaven along with a full one-third of the angels. Think about that: One-third of heaven somehow, for some reason, revolted against God. This is *really* when sin entered in. Before the garden, before the Tree of the Knowledge of Good and Evil, sin occurred in the form of rebellion. And it happened in heaven of all places—in the very presence of God.

Do you remember when sin entered into your story? Maybe it was the first time you *really* got in trouble with your parents? Maybe it was the first time you lied ... and got caught? Maybe it was the first time you swore? Or the time you stole the oversized softball from the Knock the Bottles Down game at Santa Cruz beach boardwalk ... anyone ... just me? Unfortunately, that wasn't the first time that I got in real trouble with my parents.

I remember in third grade getting really mad at my mom for some outrageous thing she had said, something like, "Son, it's time to do your homework" or "Will you come empty the dishwasher?" While I don't recall my exact response, I do remember getting so upset that I yelled at her. I believe I even used a swear word. (This was new ground for me in the third grade; I didn't know which tense to use with which word and which ones were verbs and which were nouns.) I was just so mad that I had to split. I grabbed a couple of granola bars and a Capri Sun and ran away.

I wasn't quite sure where I was going to go or how far the nearest train tracks were for me to jump in a boxcar and make my way to

Santa Fe. So I ran around the corner of our street to the property that was behind our house, where there was a huge umbrella tree that I knew I could hide out in. The umbrella tree gave me the perfect cover to elude the cops or search dogs or private investigators that my parents had no doubt hired by this point. So I sat there for the better part of fifteen minutes, stewing in my righteous indignation. I even said a few more swears to see how they would sound and to decide which ones I would need for my new life on the run. I ate a granola bar, finished the Capri Sun, and began to do some serious soul-searching. Was I really cut out for life on the road? Was I ready to live off the land and depend on the kindness of strangers? Was I wearing a coat or even a windbreaker in case it got cold? And why did I only grab granola bars and a Capri Sun?

In a moment of introspective realization and repentance, I came to my senses and decided to make the long journey home. I came through the front door like a long lost prodigal son finally returning home ... after being gone for twenty minutes. But nothing. My mom was still making dinner. Not only had she not noticed my return, but she never knew I left! She simply asked me to apologize for how I spoke to her ... and to come empty the dishwasher.

My little "swear journey" that afternoon was actually the beginning of a much bigger journey. A journey into all of the things in my life that would come *between* me and God. Little white lies, hidden habits, broken promises, broken hearts, cheap substitutes for unconditional love—you name it. Sin entered into my story and continues to come between me and God. While the details are different, your story is just the same. Sin has entered into your story and continues to come between you and God. You cannot run away from it. It's already here ... and it's already a part of who you are.

One of the most important steps you can take in your journey with God is to realize that sin isn't simply some powerful force *out there*, but rather *in here*. That there will always be a part of you that tries to come between you and God. That I am not just drawn *to* sin, but often times, compelled *by* it. This is the internal struggle of BETWEEN. This is the struggle of the Old Testament. This is the struggle that Paul speaks of in Romans 7:7–25 when he says that the desires to follow God and to forget God both occupy the same space in his heart. In other words, the struggle is real. But new life and real growth are possible once you are willing to name it, face it, refuse to run away from it, and begin to invite God into it.

This was something Lucifer refused to do, and it drove him to rebel, which drove him right out of heaven. But he was not finished! While the rest of heaven began picking up the pieces and getting back to their work of praising God, Lucifer was getting to work planning his next attack. But the next time he would attack God where it hurt Him most. He would not attack God directly, but rather those whom God loved and created.

Hiding from God (Genesis 3)

The temptation of Adam and Eve was really a retaliation. The angel fallen from heaven found a way on the earth to attack God on high. It was his attempt at revenge. Even though his plan would ultimately fail, you and I continue as casualties to this very day. The seed of sin spawned in that heavenly rebellion would take root here on the earth through that temptation in the garden.

While the timeline between the fall of Lucifer and the fall of humanity is unclear, we know that there was at least a moment unmarred by the brutality of sin. There was a relationship undivided by the separation sin brings. That took place in Eden. That relationship was between God and us. As it was in heaven, so it was on the earth: perfect, peace, unmarred beauty, undivided relationship, nothing between.

We do not know how long it existed like this. We have no idea how long it took for Lucifer to plan his attack. But what we do know is that the events of the temptation of Adam and Eve bear remarkable resemblance to the rebellious rants that Lucifer himself hurled at God. Only this time he would be more seductive, more deceptive—and in some ways, more effective. Look at what happens in the beginning of Genesis 3:

Now the serpent was more crafty than any of the wild animals the LORD God had made. He said to the woman, "Did God really say, 'You must not eat from any tree in the garden'?"

The woman said to the serpent, "We may eat fruit from the trees in the garden, but God did say, 'You must not eat fruit from the tree that is in the middle of the garden, and you must not touch it, or you will die.'"

"You will not certainly die," the serpent said to the woman. "For God knows that when you eat from it your eyes will be opened, and *you will be like God*, knowing good and evil." (Gen. 3:1–5, italics added)

"You will be like God." That phrase is the beginning of life in between. It is the sometimes subtle, other times consuming assumption that God is not enough for me. It is the belief that God is holding out on me, that God cannot be trusted. Therefore, I will do His job for Him. I will determine for myself what is right and wrong. I will live by my own rules. I will get what I want when I want. I will take what I want when I need to. I will be like God.

If that sounds familiar, it's because it's not the first time we've heard it. This was Lucifer's battle cry. What he screamed in the kingdom of heaven, he whispered in a garden on earth. And with that whisper, the separation began.

Adam and Eve believed the lie that God had held out on them and that He was not enough for them, so they ate fruit from the Tree of the Knowledge of Good and Evil. Whether that tree was literal or metaphorical, the effects were undeniable. Their eyes *were* opened, and they saw something that they had never seen before: a space between them and God. They saw and experienced something new: the separation that sin brings. And with their new eyes they saw something else that no one on earth had ever seen: shame. Shame is one of the greatest forms of self-inflicted sabotage and one of the most consistent things to come between us and God. Adam and Eve *knew* what they did was wrong, and they attempted to run and hide from God.

Genesis 3:8–11 paints the picture:

Then the man and his wife heard the sound of the LORD God as he was walking in the garden in the cool of the day, and they hid from the LORD God among the trees of the garden. But the LORD God called to the man, "Where are you?"

He answered, "I heard you in the garden, and I was afraid because I was naked; so I hid."

And he said, "Who told you that you were naked? Have you eaten from the tree that I commanded you not to eat from?"

Those words "Who told you...?" are both poignant and painful. This is the all-knowing God asking a question to which He already knew the answer. "Who told you? Who has come between you and Me? Who has told you something other than what I have already told you ... that you are my beloved son and daughter ... that you are free ... that you have all that you need ... that you can trust me?"

Recently I was reading through these verses in an early morning time of prayer and reflection and, quite unexpectedly, I began to cry. There I was, sitting in Starbucks at 5:45 a.m., crying over a moment that happened so long ago. I couldn't help but read this passage through the eyes of a parent. I couldn't imagine that feeling as a parent to have our kids, whom we have poured our heart and soul into, turn their backs on me. And run from me, hide from me, and confuse love with fear. Maybe you are a parent who has had to face a child turning their back on you—a child who despite your best efforts and attempts to love them chose to run and rebel. The sleepless nights. The hot tears that eventually run dry. The longing. The waiting. You don't need to imagine what it must have been like for God in that moment ... you already know.

Sitting in that Starbucks, I was overwhelmed with the sadness of that separation. My heart as a parent was somehow in touch and aware of what was lost in Genesis 3 that it actually began to break for God. I felt compassion ... for God. Tears formed and flowed for how sin had broken what He loved ... and knowing that in the greater story of God, this would not be the last time that sin would break someone whom God loves.

Ultimately, I suppose my heart was breaking for myself and for what has been lost in my own story. For how my sin and my choices have separated me from God. Who told *me* that *I* was naked? Who told me that *I* had to live in shame? Who told me that *I* should hide? When were those things first whispered into *my* ears? And why, at times to this very day, do I find myself still running, hiding, living in fear and shame?

A surface reading of Genesis 1 and 2 shows the relational dynamic that exists between God and humanity. Even that word, "humanity," does injustice to the intimacy of the Creator(s) and Creation, of Father and Children. While the separation of sin and what came between us and God is profoundly theological, it is also quite personal. From that moment in the garden, our terms of engagement with God would change. We see an intimacy in the garden that is almost too real to imagine. The presence of God was just that—present. God was there, with Adam and Eve, in the garden. There was no need for prayer. No wondering what God's will is for your life. No distance. No separation. But sin came between all of that and locked everyone out. Leaving all who would live in this world so close to home, but always unable to enter.

No one likes that feeling, the feeling of being locked out.

I remember the first time I became aware of that feeling. My older brothers, Scott and Justin, and I had gone out to run some errands and came back home, only to realize that we had locked ourselves out of the house. Scott (who is older than Justin and I) went quickly to solution mode: "We're gonna need to break in." He said it so quickly—almost too quickly, as if he had done this before. Hopefully, I thought, only at our house.

The three of us walked around the house to see if there were any windows that might have been left open or unlocked. We found one. It just so happened to be the window to Scott's room. We also found that the side door to our attached garage was open. This was our lucky break. If we could find a screwdriver in the garage, we could pry the screen off of Scott's window, slide the window open, and climb in.

After no luck finding a flathead screwdriver in the garage, Scott had a stroke of genius! He remembered that he had recently used the screwdriver to replace a light switch faceplate and must have left it in his room. He was right—there it was, on his desk. "If we can get that flathead in my room, we can pop this screen and get into the house!" Scott said. He continued with his revised plan: "Justin, see if the garage door to the house is open. If it is, you can get into my room and grab the screwdriver and bring it to me. Make sense?" It sure made sense to me ... but then again, I was nine years old.

Justin walked into the garage and made his way to the interior door that led to the house. Much to his surprise ... it was unlocked! Apparently in all the screen-popping, window-hopping excitement, we never bothered to check if that door was actually unlocked. Justin then proceeded, according to the plan, to walk into the house and into Scott's room. Once inside, he grabbed the screwdriver and held it up as if to say, "This one?" Scott nodded. Justin walked slowly out of the house, back through the garage to the side yard, where we were waiting for him—each step coming down like a piece of a puzzle falling in to place.

Justin handed Scott the screwdriver with a perplexed look on his face. Scott wasted no time. He popped the screen off, slid the window open, and hoisted me up to climb inside. Just like that, I was in. Scott's plan worked! We had successfully broken in ... to our unlocked house! I walked back out through the same garage door that Justin had just used and yelled with great enthusiasm, "We're in!"

This is where the story of BETWEEN begins in Genesis 3: Locked Out. Except that in Genesis 3 there's no magic screwdriver ... and no unchecked or unlocked door. Sin locked this world out from the intention of creation. Adam and Eve are locked out of paradise. And every person in the rest of the Old Testament is locked out of the intimate proximity of the presence of God that they once knew. You might even feel as if you've been living your life locked out of the life that God created you for. So close, yet so far away. Sadly, for those who lived in the days between, there would be no breaking back in. The closeness of the garden would become a distant memory.

BETWEEN the Lines

To better understand the greater story of the Bible, it might be helpful to explore the significant events of the Old Testament through the lens of its Small Word: BETWEEN. When you zoom out a bit and look at all of the different and sometimes seemingly disparate stories, moments, and characters through the greater context of BETWEEN, it might actually bring more clarity and connectedness.

This is what sets in motion the events of the Old Testament. This moment in the garden serves as the opening lines of the rest of the Old Testament. This is where BETWEEN begins. So with that backstory in mind, let's look at major events and movements of the Old Testament through the lens of BETWEEN. I pray as you do that stories you may have never heard before, or stories that you may have heard so often that they've lost their meaning, are given new light and life by the God who gave them to us. And that you might not only have a greater understanding of the Old Testament, but a greater love for the God who time and again goes between us and our sin.

Covenants and Commandments
(Genesis 9 to Exodus 25)

Early in the story of the Old Testament we see God coming between us and the separation that sin brought by making covenants or promises with His people. A covenant is a contract of sorts, a guarantee in which God says to His people, "When all else fails around you, you can always count on Me."

In the presence and perfection of the garden, there was no need for covenants. All was as it should be. However, several generations after sin enters in, God steps in BETWEEN us and our sin and makes a significant covenant with one of the last holy and honest people on earth at that time: Noah. In Genesis 6:18, God promises to save Noah's family from the flood that He is bringing to the earth and to begin anew with them. God keeps His covenant. Shortly after the Flood, God continues in His covenant to Noah and says,

> "I now establish my covenant with you and with your descendants after you.... I establish my covenant with you: Never again will all life be destroyed by the waters of a flood; never again will there be a flood to destroy the earth." (Gen. 9:9, 11)

God goes on to give a sign to seal the deal of the covenant — a rainbow (Gen. 9:13–16) — so that every time Noah and his family and their descendants see it, they will be reminded that God is faithful. God came between the depravity of the world and the destruction of the world through the deliverance of Noah, because God always keeps His covenant.

But perhaps the most famous covenant is between God and Abraham. God makes a promise to Abraham in Genesis 15 that He will form a nation through his offspring. A nation. Try and imagine hearing those words. How does one go about having a nation? Can you imagine the conversation between Abraham and one of his neighbors?

> "Abraham, my friend, good to see you! What do you and Sarah have planned this weekend?"
>
> "Not much, really. Some chores around the tent, mostly dusting. Maybe a little antiquing, which we call shopping. Oh,... and it looks like the Mrs. and I are going to make a nation ... so there's that. You?"

This is obviously a *big* promise that God was making to Abraham. God was committing to doing something for Abraham that Abraham could never do for himself. God was promising him not only a nation, but also a child. Just one child was more than Abraham and Sarah expected, based on their age and stage of life. They had tried for years, even decades, to have a child ... but were unable. They watched their friends and family have children and their children have children, but there were no children for Abraham and Sarah. Yet, once again God goes between all that we see for ourselves and all that He sees for us.

Even then, Abraham still questions the character of God. In Genesis 15:2–3, Abraham asks,

> "Sovereign LORD, what can you give me since I remain childless and the one who will inherit my estate is Eliezer of Damascus? [Abraham's servant]" And Abram said, "You have given me no children; so a servant in my household will be my heir."

Do you see the extent to which sin had separated? The God of the universe who created life from nothing only a handful of generations prior is being called to task by Abraham to make sure that He is a God of His word. It's a bold and brutally honest move on Abraham's part. He wants to know if God will really do it. If God will hold up His end of the bargain. If God's promise is good.

Even in the absence of Abraham's trust, God still makes His covenant. Sarah did become pregnant, against all odds, and gave birth to Isaac. Isaac became the father of Jacob, and Jacob the father of twelve sons, each of whom would form his own tribe. Together those tribes became the eventual nation of Israel. Within a few short generations, God's promise to Abraham was fulfilled. God always keeps His covenants.

With each and every covenant kept, God established a trail of goodness and faithfulness—a way for us to trace thousands of years of promises kept. While Noah and Abraham and the Israelites could only see what pertained to them in that moment, we see over the fullness of time the faithfulness of God. With each covenant, God stands between our *Now* and His *Not Yet*. He bridges the gap between our *Here* and His *There* time and again, because God always keeps His covenant.

Few things clarify and magnify the faithfulness of God like good old desperation. When you can see no other way but God, it becomes much easier to recognize His faithfulness. When Jeanne and I were leaving our Dream Life in Atlanta to start Soul City Church in

Chicago … we were desperate. We had cashed *everything* in to start this church and wouldn't be receiving a salary for what would turn out to be eighteen months.

One day, while still in Atlanta, sitting on the floor in the middle of a house full of boxes, Jeanne began to write out to God her desperate plea for His faithfulness. Our home has always meant so much to us. It is both our place of refuge and rest as well as ground zero for how we serve God and love others. We *love* our home. We loved the home we had built in Atlanta and were afraid we would never have anything like that again. So Jeanne decided to get *real* specific with God. She wrote out, in detail, all that she wanted to see Him provide in a home … down to the basement … down to the window over the sink in the kitchen … down to a modern open floor plan. She spared no detail. She figured that if God was both good and faithful, why not ask? With tears still soaking through several pages, she closed her prayer journal and packed it away in a box.

Several weeks after we moved to Chicago, Jeanne and I finally unpacked the box that held her journal. As she stood in our new kitchen, looking out through the window above our sink, in the midst of a modern open-floor-plan house, with a fully carpeted basement, and a bedroom for each of our kids, she began to let tears soak that journal once more. God had done it. He had been more faithful than we could have even imagined.

You see, the home that God so perfectly provided for us was not the home that we had chosen. Just five days before moving to Chicago, we lost the rental home for which we had signed a lease. The moving trucks were already at the house we were moving out of in Atlanta. So in that desperate moment, we did what anyone would do: We went to Craigslist! Within twenty-four hours we signed a lease to a house that we had only seen in eleven pictures. By that weekend we were living in that home!

God is faithful. We are forgetful. This is the story of the Old Testament and so often the stories of our life with God. We forget how faithful He is. God's covenant faithfulness is not only meant to grow our faith, but to remind us of the faith that we once had. It simultaneously moves us forward ... while taking us back.

In the same way that the covenants stand between our forgetfulness and God's faithfulness, the Ten Commandments stand between our wayward wandering and God's loving leadership. In the garden, Adam and Eve walked and talked with God. He was present and shared in their work (Gen. 2:19–20). But in the separation brought about by sin, God's daily dynamic direction becomes a thing of the past. And so God once again helps bridge the gap— goes BETWEEN—by giving the Ten Commandments as a guide through the distance created by sin.

The Ten Commandments are a significant symbol of the time *between* sin and salvation. Rather than a to-do list left by a spouse or parent before heading off for a business trip, these commandments were given by God to be a way to live *with* Him. A way to live your life in this world that blesses God, is good for you, and draws the attention of the world around you. This is what the Ten Commandments and the more than 600 laws found in Leviticus, Numbers, and Deuteronomy consistently point to: a way of living *with* God in the lack of His discernible presence.

Over time, spiritual leaders would scrutinize and systematize, would boil down and beef up, each and every letter of the law in an attempt at holiness that ultimately lacked the heart of God. All along the way, they were missing the point that the laws and commandments were never actually the point! The Ten Commandments and all of the laws found in the Old Testament were never intended to be a source of salvation, but rather a way *between* God's loving daily guidance in a world overrun by sin. To prove that point, hundreds of years later, Jesus would sum up every letter of every law and commandment with this one simple but life-changing idea:

> Love God with all of who you are....
> Love others like you love yourself.
> (Matt. 22:37, 39 paraphrased)

Love is what it was always all about. Every letter of every law was written in love—loving God, loving others, loving your life. This is the point. Every covenant and commandment is an act of a God going before and *between* His people and their sin. It is how He lovingly led them every step of the way through the desert of their sin. Between their nows and His not yets. Between their sin and His salvation.

Tabernacles, Temples, and Priests (Exodus 25 to Judges 1)

Suppose a stranger were to interrupt you right now, while you were reading this book, and ask you completely out of the blue, "Where is God?" What would you say—other than, "Do I know you?" How would you respond? My hunch is that most of us might say something like, "God is everywhere" or "God is in heaven." Maybe you would say, "God is in my heart." It's a simple question, but how you answer it really matters and reveals something about how you view God.

This question reminds me of the story of two young brothers at a small country church in rural Alabama. A new pastor had come to this church and wanted to meet all of the children in Sunday school. The two brothers met outside the door of his meager office in the back of the church. The older brother went in first. The door closed behind him. The pastor strolled about his office, eyeing the boy, and then, in an ever so intimidating voice, asked him, "Son,... where is Gaawwd?" The boy sat speechless. "Where is ... Gaawwd?" the pastor repeated in a passionate preacher's tone.

The boy got so scared in that moment that, in a panic, he eyed the open window that overlooked the gravel parking lot outside, ran straight for it, and jumped through and hid in the bushes just below. The pastor, quite confused, called for the younger brother to come in. The first thing the boy noticed was his missing brother. The second thing was the pacing pastor. Sweat began to form on the boy's little brow. The pastor asked the same question, "Son,...

Where is ... Gaawwd?" The boy's eyes doubled in size. "Where ... is ... Gaawwd?" the pastor asked again just like before.

Instinctively, the boy did exactly what his brother had done moments earlier. He ran for the window and quickly climbed out. When he landed in the bushes, he was surprised to see his brother hiding there. He quickly blurted out, "This ain't good! God's gone missing ... and they think *we* had something to do with it!"

"Where is God?" Ask this question of just about any Israelite in the Old Testament from Moses on down, and the answer would be something like, "The Almighty dwells in the tabernacle." Or later in their story, "The Lord dwells in the temple, in the Holy of Holies." In the Old Testament, the people of God actually built a place for God to dwell. Think about that for a moment. The God who created everything, had a place created for Himself to dwell. So great was the effect of sin in and on this world that God couldn't even be among people anymore, lest His holiness consume and overwhelm them and ultimately destroy them (Ex. 33:5). So the people of God, instructed by God, built the tabernacle and later the temple—physical spaces for a spiritual being to dwell. It was as though the people of God needed a reminder, some sort of assurance that God was *with* them. And this is precisely what the tabernacle and temple came to serve as—a physical reminder of God's spiritual presence.

The tabernacle was built by Moses and the Israelites (Ex. 25), with God serving as the architect and foreman on the project. He gave Moses specific instructions and dimensions on how it should be built, down to size, building material, and decor. It was essentially a portable tent and courtyard where *only* the priests were allowed to go. But the priests could only go so far. Only the high priest was allowed to enter the Holy of Holies—once a year (on the day of Atonement). So in the actual place where God "dwelled" in the Old Testament, only one person was allowed to enter that one space, one day per year.

Years later, the temple would follow suit. King David, compelled by his trusted advisor Nathan, came up with a plan to turn the mobile home of the tabernacle into a permanent palace for God. Seeing the blood underneath David's fingernails from years of war, God told

David that his grand vision of the temple would come to pass, but not in his lifetime. It was Solomon, David's son, who would go on to build the temple. Solomon essentially took everything that was at the essence of the tabernacle and supersized it, right down to the Holy of Holies.

Once again, an omnipresent God chose to make His presence known, but in only one room that only one person in the entire nation could ever enter—on one day out of the year. Like the tabernacle before it, the temple was the answer to the question, "Where is God?" God lived in the temple. God was right over there—right in that room that no one could get to. Present … but seemingly distant. God was close—but you couldn't see Him. You couldn't get to Him. Whereas Adam and Eve enjoyed long walks with God in wide-open spaces in the garden, the people of God throughout the Old Testament would have to settle for a room.

It's amazing to read in 1 Kings all the outstanding and ornate and outrageously expensive detail that went into the temple. Had Liberace been around in those days, even he might have said, "Now that's a bit much." Every gold wall and marble courtyard, every giant door and veiled curtain was a reminder that this God was close—but that was as close as you could get. The tabernacle and the temple were how God chose to go *between* His all-consuming holiness and our ever-growing sinfulness. This physical space was the approximate proximity between divinity and humanity.

Temple worship was at that time the God-given strategy for offloading the weight of sin in their lives. It was an intentional, sometimes elaborate system of sacrifices offered at specific times over the course of a year. Some sacrifices were offered for individuals, some for families, some for the whole nation. Some were offered at several points throughout the year; some were offered only once. This wasn't as much for God … as it was for us. Each sacrifice and celebration was lovingly crafted by God to heal the people's hearts and to demonstrate that despite whatever sin stood *between*, God's love was greater. It was to remind the people of God of the faithfulness of God and to prepare them for the ultimate sacrifice that was to come.

This system of sacrifices made sense in the time of BETWEEN. But just like commandments and the tabernacle and temple, the sacrifice itself was not the point. It was the heart behind the sacrifice that God was most interested in. The system and strategy of sacrifices that God implemented in the Old Testament were meant to prepare someone's heart for God to come between. It was how we connect with a God who had been distanced by our sin. It was the way to be present with God, even if you couldn't be face to face as Adam and Eve once were.

I love the idea of being able to be present, even when you're distant. I love being able to see and connect with our kids when I happen to be away overnight. All of that is great. It's just the rebuffering that I hate, that lag time where I have to stare at a frozen face asking over and over again, "Are you there? I'm not seeing you ... can you hear me? I didn't get that part...." — only to hear back, "I ... signal ... hold ... wi-fi ... umlaut ... tango ... bravo." For that reason, I have personally never been a very big fan of tools like Skype or Facetime. I feel as if I spend half my time on Skype awkwardly smiling, waiting for a response from the other end, while trying not to look as if I'm staring at the little square that has my face in it to make sure my hair looks good. The lag time is the worst part.

Yet when it comes to the sin that gets between me and God, I can easily spend a long time in lag time. Like the weeks and months of space between the feasts, festivals, and sacrifices in the original temple system, there tends to be a lot of lag time between committing my sin and confessing my sin. I imagine God on the other end saying, "Hey! Can you hear Me? I said I love you. Did you get that? I will forgive you ... *forgive you!*" I wonder how much of the suffering that comes from my sin is due not only to the committing, but also the carrying.

If you were to stop right now and spend five minutes examining your heart, playing back the tapes from the past couple weeks — how much unconfessed sin do you think you might find? How far back might it go? How long have you been living in a lag time with God? How much do you think it has affected and infected your soul? How might it have impacted your relationships with others? What about your relationship with God? Do you think that there might be a better strategy for our sin?

A few years ago I had the opportunity to co-teach with my friend John at a church retreat. I can't recall what it was we were teaching on, but I'll never forget what he said in response to an impromptu question from the audience at the end of our teaching time. Someone asked, "If I'm really growing in my relationship with God, why aren't I sinning any less?"

John paused, then answered with this: "What I'm discovering about spiritual growth is that it isn't just about sinning less ... although we all probably should try to sin less ... but rather, it's about shortening the gap between my *sin* and my *confession*." Let me repeat that: Spiritual growth isn't merely about sinning less, but about shortening the lag time between sin and confession.

The longer I choose to carry around my sin, the farther I extend the gap BETWEEN God and me—between sin and confession, between burden and freedom, between death and life. God has ultimately settled the gap through Jesus. The only gap that remains is the one that you and I create when we choose to sit in our sin—or to stay stuck, to stew, to settle for life at a distance from God. Is there anything right now that you are carrying that God never asked you to carry? Any hidden pattern of sin that you are currently managing? Anything that you are convinced God cannot free you from? Any moment of sin from your past that you may have asked God to forgive, but you keep the tapes of shame and regret stuck on repeat? Did you blow up at your spouse this morning and out of some stubborn sense of pride refuse to ask God and the love of your life to forgive you? Are you currently harboring a deep feeling of jealousy and envy over your friend who recently got engaged while you remain single? What are you carrying that is keeping you from God ... and how much longer do you intend to carry it?

What would it look like for you to shorten the gap and ask for forgiveness right now? To put down this book and go to the right person (Jesus and your spouse, friend, sister, co-worker, etc.) at the right time (now) in the right place (here) and ask for the forgiveness that leads to freedom. To not wait till the end of the day or the end of your rope or the end of your life to settle your account with God. How can you, today, practice keeping short accounts with God?

When I was nineteen, a childhood friend whom I had grown up with was killed quite unexpectedly. His death came as quite a shock to us all, most understandably to his parents. I will never forget having a conversation with his dad, months after the tragedy, when he was still engulfed in the all-encompassing fog of grief. Fumbling for words, I asked how he was holding up, and while I'm not quite sure how I expected him to respond, I'll never forget what he said. "Keep short accounts, Jarrett. Keep short accounts with God. With the people you love. Don't ever let anything stand between you and the people you love. You never know how long you've got."

Keep short accounts. When it comes to the gap between my sin and my confession, there is simply no good reason to wait. No special day you have to wait for. No special place you have to go. No priest that you need to do it for you. You are not bound by those things. And you are not bound by your sin. You see, the good news is that there is nothing that can separate you from the love of God. Nothing! Today can truly be the day today that you shorten the gap *between* sin and your confession ... *between* you and God.

Judges and Kings (Judges 1 to II Chronicles 36)

The Israelites give us a great window into the relentless wants and restless wanderings of our souls. It seems as though, no matter what God gave them, eventually they wanted *more*. Even though God had given them the temple and priests as a way BETWEEN, as a way to be with God in the presence of sins' separation—still they wanted more. They began gazing at the greener grasses of their neighbor nations. They all seemed to have something that Israel did not ... something that they desperately desired ... a king!

The people of God had grown in number. They had acquired more and more land and were becoming more and more spread out.

So God gave them judges to guide and guard them. These were God's "go-to" leaders whose job it was to remind the people of God of His purpose. But that wasn't enough, because they wanted a *king*! First Samuel 8 gives us a window into their wanting and whining. Samuel was the last of the judges ... only he didn't know that yet when the people approached him.

> They said to him, "You are old, and your sons do not follow your ways; now appoint a king to lead us, such as all the other nations have."
>
> But when they said, "Give us a king to lead us," this displeased Samuel; so he prayed to the Lord. And the Lord told him: "Listen to all that the people are saying to you; it is not you they have rejected, but they have rejected me as their king. As they have done from the day I brought them up out of Egypt until this day, forsaking me and serving other gods, so they are doing to you. Now listen to them; but warn them solemnly and let them know what the king who will reign over them will claim as his rights." (vv. 5 – 9)

The people of God wanted to be like all of the other people they saw around them. They saw a king as a symbol of status, as their validation, as the solution to all their problems. What they failed to see was the oppression that kings tend to bring with them. They failed to see that often the first line in a king's job description was: "Rule over people."

The people of God had never been "ruled over" by anyone up to this point, and now they were rejecting God as their one true King. So God decided to let them have their way — not as an act of giving up, but rather as giving over. He gave His people over to their desire to have something ... anything other than Him. The great twist in this significant section of the Old Testament is not that God was going *between* His people and their sin, but that *they* were placing something *between* God and them. It is an echo of that ancient lie whispered in the Garden, that God was holding out on them and ultimately that He was not enough.

Not surprisingly, the Great King Experiment failed and ended up dividing and destroying what it was supposed to protect and reign and rule over. There were bright spots, however (see King David and his son Solomon), but they were the exception. There were 41 kings and one queen who ruled over Israel and Judah (the Southern Kingdom that was divided from Israel during the time of the kings). Of the 42 royal rulers of Israel and Judah, only 10 can be considered "good."

Those aren't great odds. Think of it this way: 75 percent of the kings and queens who ruled over the people of God were not only "bad"; some were downright evil! But more than that, 100 percent of the kings that ruled over Israel and Judah serve as yet another reminder of the distance that sin creates between God and us. These rulers are just another example of what we do and what we look to in an attempt to fill the space BETWEEN.

With King Envy as a part of Israel's story, it's no surprise that when Jesus came, many tried to make Him a king. They fashioned Him as the New David, there to overthrow their oppressors and reestablish Israel to its former forgotten glory. But what those first followers of Jesus could not possibly perceive was that He was so much more of a king than they could have ever begged or bargained for. King Jesus would establish and rule over a new kingdom that would never end—an upside-down kingdom that brings heaven to earth. A kingdom that stands in peaceful protest to the kingdoms of this world. Jesus is a King who gives us so much more than what everyone else around us already has, but He gives us what everyone else around us so desperately needs.

The Psalms—The Soul of Separation

In the middle of the Old Testament you will find its soul: the gut-wrenchingly honest, fear-filled, faith-filled, sometimes poetic, sometimes frantic book of Psalms. A psalm is basically a prayer set to music. It is intended for both private reflection and communal expression. Some psalms are short and simple, and some are long and profound. Despite their unique distinctions and intentions, all 150 of them are a perfect picture of the soul of the Old Testament. They are what it feels like to be living in BETWEEN. In fact, the writers of the Psalms often speak directly to and about the soul.

> Why, my soul, are you downcast?
>> Why so disturbed within me?
> Put your hope in God,
>> for I will yet praise him,
>> my Savior and my God. (Ps. 43:5)
> Truly my soul finds rest in God;
>> my salvation comes from him. (Ps. 62:1)
> Praise the LORD, my soul;
>> all my inmost being,
>> praise his holy name.
> Praise the LORD, my soul,
>> and forget not all his benefits. (Ps. 103:1–2)

The writers of the Psalms have no problem shifting from hands raised to God in adoration to fingers pointed at God in accusation. One minute the psalmist will be declaring the loving goodness of God, the next giving vivid detail to how he wants to extract revenge on all of his enemies and how he thinks God can help!

Notice in Psalm 143:12 how comfortably the psalmist moves from God's love to God leveling all his foes:

> In your unfailing love, silence my enemies;
>> destroy all my foes,
>> for I am your servant.

The writers of the Psalms also give us a compelling if not uncomfortable picture of what brokenness and confession look like. David especially does not hold back in naming his sin and how it has come *between* him and God. His raw and vulnerable confession has given me the words to say to God when I find the courage to confess. Psalm 51 in particular has been a "go-to" psalm for me for the better part of the last twenty years. Listen to the sound of a soul coming clean:

Have mercy on me, O God,
    according to your unfailing love;
according to your great compassion
    blot out my transgressions.
Wash away all my iniquity
    and cleanse me from my sin.
For I know my transgressions,
    and my sin is always before me. (Ps. 51:1–3)

Look at this utterly honest, end-of-the-rope request to God found in Psalm 51:12 and see if these words are similar to prayers that you may have prayed in your most honest and depleted moments:

Restore to me the joy of your salvation
    and grant me a willing spirit, to sustain me.

If you ever want to know what it feels like to live in the space BETWEEN OF and WITH, look no further than the Psalms. If you want a picture of what your soul looks like, look no further than the Psalms. The Psalms are the soul's EKG—a written read-out of what's really going on. They give us not only a historical reflection of what it was like for them then, but also what it is like for us now. How often does my soul swing from deep love and connectedness with God to an insatiable selfishness and insecurity? How often do you honestly come to God wanting to thank Him for who He is and what He's done, only to find yourself rattling off your prewritten list of all that you want Him to do for you (including but not limited to vanquishing your enemies)?

The Psalms are a gift from God in that they hold a mirror up to our soul and give us words to name what is often unseen. They remind us that life with God is real and raw and beautiful and broken—and that we too are invited to pour our soul out to God. Nothing needs to be polished up or edited down. God not only can handle it, but ultimately desires it!

Prophets (Isaiah 1 to Malachi 4)

The kings of the Old Testament would eventually lead the people of God to ruin, and in the rubble of their rejection of God, He brings a way BETWEEN … yet again. Toward the end of the rule of kings, God decided to send His people His prophets. The prophets, similar to the judges before them, spoke on behalf of God, to the people of God, about the heart of God. Not surprisingly, their passionate pleas often fell on deaf ears.

The Major and Minor Prophets who occupy the pages of the last quarter of the Old Testament were each different and unique in their own way. They had varied styles, approaches, and effectiveness. Yet they all shared one common message: "Repent! Seriously! We mean it. Repent! God's not messing around!" The prophets were God's final appeal to His people before going silent for a time.

The prophets, like the judges before them, were the people God sent to stand in the gap *between* depravity and divinity. They were the mouthpieces for God. However, unlike their predecessors, the kings, they were not voices of the people's choosing. Prophets such as Elijah, Isaiah, Jeremiah, and Jonah were those God chose to get His people's attention. Like mediators at a negotiation table, God's representatives did their best, but by this point, the people's ears were too clogged and their hearts too hardened.

And it's not as if they didn't try. They did all that they could to get the people's attention. Isaiah stripped down and walked around naked (Isa. 20). Jeremiah was a streaking prophet too, only the Bible says that he hid his underwear for a "long time" (Jer. 13). Then Jonah, after seeing God spare the city of Nineveh from destruction, threw a complete fit and begged God to kill him … just days after God had spared his life by delivering him from the belly of a giant fish (Jonah 4). Then there was Hosea, who married a prostitute as an "object lesson" to one of his sermons. And Ezekiel, who, after seeing a vision from God and receiving a scroll with God's commands written on it, ate that scroll down to the very last letter.

The prophets did whatever God asked them to get the attention and win back the hearts of the Israelites—but it all seemed in vain. No matter what God did to go between His people and their sin, they simply wouldn't listen anymore.

So, after the prophet Malachi made his passionate plea for the people to turn their hearts back to God, God decided to go silent. For 400 years there wasn't a single new commandment or new covenant. God's voice couldn't be heard through priest or prophet, judge, or king. All the years and years of God's relentless effort to get the people's attention led to a deafening silence.

While the Old Testament began with a BANG, it ends on a much more melancholy note that punctuates the power and presence of the space that sin created BETWEEN us and God. The story of the Old Testament began with the words "It is good," but the feeling at the end is that "all was lost." However, what 400 years could not convey is that this was not the end of the story. This temporary silence would lead to a permanent solution: One who would forevermore bridge the space BETWEEN.

Conclusion: The Story Continues ... Even When Nothing Is Happening

Living in the Midwest as long as I have, I have come to appreciate the seasons. Where I grew up in northern California, we only had one season: "Awesome." Yes, 365 days of "Awesome!" When we lived in Georgia, we quickly learned that there are three seasons: "Pollen," "Hot," "SEC Football." But here in the Midwest, we have all four seasons. Each of them has its place and purpose. The one that Midwesterners talk about most (and by that I mean *complain* about the most) is Winter. Ask anyone here in Chicago, and they will tell you that winter always comes way too early and lasts far too long.

Technically, in the Midwest winter is only supposed to last from mid-December to mid-March, but last year it snowed on Halloween. Really! Do you know how hard it is to see a kid dressed like a ghost in the middle of a snowstorm? Winter in the Midwest can be brutal. During my first winter in Chicago I couldn't get over how my nose hairs would freeze. I didn't even know that was a thing. But apparently it is. Every year, winter comes, and just about everything in nature closes up shop and hangs a sign in the window saying, "Be Back in April."

With everything being dark and cold during winter, it's easy to assume that in nature nothing is happening, but that couldn't be any further from the truth. Trees, for example, go into dormancy. They literally slow their metabolism down during the coldest months (which is also a practice I hold during those months) and stay alive by living more simply and exerting less energy. They stop growing branches and leaves to save energy for when it's the right time to grow. Any arborist worth their weight in acorns will tell you that if you keep a tree from the process of dormancy, you actually limit its growth and lifespan. In other words, this annual shutting-down is normal and necessary. Without winter, a tree is not fully ready for spring.

This is in essence what happened to the people of God after the prophet Malachi spoke his final plea ... they went dormant. They entered the final bitter months of the season known as BETWEEN. During this time, not a word was spoken by God. There were 400 years of wintry silence. There was nothing seemingly significant happening on the surface, at least nothing to write about it. But it was precisely during this time that God was silently and quietly arranging the last details for the arrival of Jesus. The silence and dormancy on the surface were only serving to make the arrival of Jesus that much more significant. It may seem as though all was quiet, but all the while, God was tying up all the loose ends of hundreds of prophecies and thousands of years of weaving and wandering and waiting. This silent season of "winter" was needed then, as it always is, for us to truly recognize spring.

I suppose the same is true of our lives. We all encounter our "winter" seasons—a season of death or loss or shattered dreams. A season of dreams deferred. A season of calling out to God, only to receive the icy silence of winter. A season when it seems as though all is lost and the story is over. Yet, if you've walked through one of those seasons in the past, the simple act of your reading these words now is proof that not *all* was lost. My hunch is that there are things that have grown in and out of you because of that dark and dormant season. Life has somehow come from that death ... as it always does.

If you happen to be in one of those seasons right now, then with all grace and as much strength as you can muster ... take heart. It may seem cold and dark and lonely. That's only because it is. Winter comes to all of us, and it needs to stay as long as it needs to stay. But just because all may seem lost or not as it should be, or not as you would like it on the surface, that doesn't mean that God is not at work behind the scenes and beneath the soil. He is working something out in you and for you that, honestly, can't be worked out in any other season.

So be present with the season that you are in. Do not mourn too long the seasons that have passed, for they *will* come again. And do not be so fixated on the next season that you miss the one that you are in right now. Just as God took care of His people through 400 years of silence, He will take care of you in this season.

Take comfort in the words that God gave to David: "Be still, and know that I am God" (Ps. 46:10). Trust that this season will last as long as is needed and will pass when the time is right. Like every season since the dawn of creation, like every single season in the Bible, and like in every story of every person who has walked through winter, remember this: God is at work. The story continues and, if you are present to it, it gets even better ... even when it seems as if nothing is happening.

4

Part Four

WITH

Matthew 1 to Acts 1

The Big Idea of the Small Word: WITH

There are four accounts of the birth, life, death, and resurrection of Jesus. They are the first four books in the New Testament: Matthew, Mark, Luke, and John. These books represent the third of the Four Small Words that tell the story of the Bible — WITH. God WITH us. So significant is this reality for us and our relationship with God that He makes sure that one of the names given to Jesus is "Immanuel" (Matt. 1:23), which literally means "God WITH us." *With* ... changed everything.

Jesus is God's living reminder that even though the world had spent generation after generation wandering through the Valley of BETWEEN, God had never left them or forgotten them. He was in fact present, even though at times He seemed distant. He was WITH them then ... and He is WITH us now.

We need *with* more than we may know. We each need the life-giving and sustaining power that comes from presence, such as people being with us. It is precisely because we are created from the community of the Trinity that we have a profound need for community with others. We simply can't live without others. In fact, researchers recently studied 6,500 men and women aged 52 and older and found that loneliness and social isolation can increase death risk by 26 percent in that season of life! In other words, our lives depend on WITH.

God knows this and demonstrated His love for us in that while we were lost and alone, pretending to be god, the one true God sent His one and only Son, Jesus, to be *with* us and offer His life *for* us.

As you read this section, consider what that must have been like for Jesus to come into this world and into our story. After 400 years of silence, after thousands of years of wandering and waiting, God not only speaks, not only moves, but comes. He comes to be *with* us, so that anyone and everyone can once again and once and for all have relationship *with* Him. God could have delivered from a distance, but He didn't. He could have settled for another substitute, but He didn't. He came to walk with us, as He once did in the Garden. To walk with us into the life that He actually created us for.

Pay special attention as you read this chapter and as we talk about the four gospel accounts of just how much Jesus lives up to the idea of Immanuel. Notice not only *how* He is with us, but *who* He was with while He walked this earth. Jesus went to those whom everyone else went out of their way to avoid. God coming to us to be with us is a tangible demonstration of the open invitation that God makes to all people to be in relationship with Him. God ended our time in BETWEEN by being WITH, and He is inviting you to respond in kind by leaving your old life of BETWEEN and entering into a new life and new relationship WITH Him.

A Long Distance

I met my wife Jeanne in the fall of 1993 during a weeklong trip to Chicago. We met for the first time at the Omni Hotel, where I was couch/vacation crashing with a friend who was on a trip to Chicago with his family. Jeanne was attending the college I was considering transferring to, and she happened to be friends with some friends I knew there. In fact, she was just starting to date one of those friends. She instantly fascinated me. She was smart, witty, strong, gorgeous, confident, and outgoing, and she loved God in such a real and beautiful way. I just had to be around her.

We ended up seeing each other several times during the week that I was visiting Chicago, and we eventually spent my last day in the city together, just the two of us. Honestly, it was like those highlight reels they have in romantic comedies set to some cheesy song from the 1980s such as "Walking on Sunshine." It was perfect. I was done. All I wanted was to be near her. But the problem was that (a) I was leaving the next morning to fly back to San Francisco, and (b) I had a girlfriend back in San Francisco whom I had been dating for almost three years.

The night before I flew out, I wrote Jeanne a thank-you note that turned into a three-page declaration of admiration. Borderline stalkerish. I told her all that I saw in her. I told her how amazed I was at who she was. I told her that I wanted to get to know her more. And ... I told her that I had a girlfriend back home. I told Jeanne that if she was interested in seeing where this would go, she could let me know.

Within days of that letter, I broke up with a great girl whom I had known since middle school. It was rough, I'll admit. In hindsight, I could have waited another week to do it, seeing that I broke up with her on her birthday (not cool!). But we're friends now on Facebook, so ...

Within a few weeks Jeanne and I began a long-distance relationship. Mind you, this was 1993. There was no Skype, no email, no texting. And cell phones cost about $7,400. So we talked on the phone. We sent letters and pictures. We would make trips every few months to see each other. We made every effort to make long distance work. And it did for about a year and a half until we hit that wall that we always saw coming: For this relationship to grow, we will have to live in the same zip code. We will need to be WITH each other. In proximity. In real time. Face to face.

After eighteen months of long distance, I made my way to Chicago. We were finally *with* each other. Not surprisingly, our relationship changed dynamically. Now we could see each other, faults and all. Now we could experience what phone calls and letters and three-day trips had never allowed. Everything changed for us once we were able to be *with* each other. We clearly had a relationship over those eighteen months of long distance, but we didn't *know* each other fully. We hadn't experienced life together.

Within a year, we were married. And at the time of my writing this, we set reservations at the Omni Hotel where we met. I was taking Jeanne back to where it all started, to celebrate twenty years of falling in love.

It is hard for us in this digital age to fully grasp the power of WITH. We are more connected than ever, but rarely face to face. I am friends with people all over the world whom I have never physically met. We chat, comment, text, tweet. We have found a way to be friends with each other without being WITH each other. While we may be losing some of the skills of actually being able to socially relate to someone, our desire for that connection has only deepened. This is why we have meet-ups. This is why online dating eventually leads to an actual date. This is why people still go to conventions and conferences in person, when they could easily grab the content online. We want WITH.

As odd as it may sound, much of the Old Testament plays out like a long-distance relationship with God. There was a relationship, and it was real. But it was constrained and defined by the very real separation of sin. God was present, but also seemed distant. The story of the Gospels is the story of how Jesus came a "long distance" to be *with* us. To break the silence and bridge the gap between us and God once and for all. To call off the long-distance relationship by moving into our town, moving into our hearts, and teaching us how to live *our* lives *with* Him. This is what God has created you for. This is what Jesus came for. And WITH is where our story with Him begins.

A Not-So-Silent Night (Matthew 1:18–25; Luke 2:1–22)

The story of the birth of Jesus is something that is celebrated, told, and retold every year all over the world. There are songs, pageants, made-for-TV movies, trinkets, and ornaments. I've even seen little statues of Santa kneeling at the manger of Jesus.

We have heard and told the story so much that somewhere along the way the details seemed to have been lost. We often remember only the poetic parts:

(1) Virgin

(2) Bethlehem

(3) No room in the inn

(4) Manger

(5) Drummer boy

(6) Three kings

Those last two aren't even a part of the actual birth account, but they always make it in anyway. And that's exactly the problem—our "familiarity" with the story has left us at a distance from the brutal and beautiful realities of the amazing story of God coming to be WITH us!

There are several often-overlooked aspects of the story that make this story more ... human. They remind us that despite the fairy-tale wrappings we put on the story every year, the account of God coming to be WITH us is as gritty as it is pretty. This story is much more "real world" than "feel good." More human ... and yet somehow more divine.

What we have come to call the good news of God coming to be *with* us through Jesus was not at first received as good. The news was as unplanned as it was unexpected for Mary and Joseph and their families and friends. Their life was simple, uncomplicated, and ... boring. They were engaged to be married in the town that Mary had grown up in. Joseph's work wasn't lucrative, but it was steady and stable ... predictable. But all that changed.

Mary was already intuitively aware that something spiritual was in the air. After years and years of infertility, her older cousin Elizabeth was suddenly pregnant. But that's not the half of it. In hushed tones behind closed doors, Elizabeth had confided in Mary that an angel of the Lord had visited her husband, Zechariah. After 400 years of silence, God had spoken—to her cousin's husband, of all people.

The angel told them that their son was to be a prophet in the spirit of Elijah and that God was calling His people back to Him. All of the prophecies that Mary had studied and heard recited in her home suddenly came flashing back to her. But not simply to her head; rather, they were finding their home in her heart. As though they were personal ... for her. And then it happened.

She was alone in her room, thumbing through that month's copy of *Hebrew Teen Bride Magazine*, when he appeared. Beautiful and terrifying all at once. She had never seen anyone or anything like it ... like this angel. Then he spoke. He spoke to her by name and told her not to be afraid (too late). He said that she was special to God and that God was *with* her. WITH ... her.

Any doubt still lingering from Elizabeth's account had suddenly vanished in the presence of this heavenly visitor. He said that she too would become pregnant and that her son's name was already picked out: Jesus. He is the One. The One that all the prophecies promised. The One that all of heaven celebrated. The One that the world had been waiting for.

Mary, now suddenly feeling a surge of confidence in this angel's presence, asked how this was ever possible. She wasn't sure if angels knew about the birds and the bees or where babies come from. She was ready to explain how this all simply wasn't possible, when the angel told her that God would *make* it possible. If God could cause her elderly cousin, who had been infertile her whole life, to become pregnant, He could certainly cause a teenager who had never had sex to become pregnant. And that's exactly what happened.

This is where the fairy tale becomes a reality show. While Mary was quick to trust God, her fiancé, Joseph, was not as inclined. This was not because he lacked faith, but because he was very faithful … to the law. The law implied that if a woman was unfaithful to her fiancé, the marriage could be called off. The husband was still entitled to his dowry from her father and would be regarded as righteous for calling off the marriage. He would be fine. She, however, would not be. The unfaithful fiancée would be scorned—an outcast unwelcome in her community and in her family. And in the case of pregnancy from infidelity, the baby's lot would be far worse.

While Joseph was faithful to the law, he also loved Mary very much, so he determined that he would divorce her quietly and spare her from as much public spectacle as possible. This is where the story was going. Mary was pregnant with the Savior of the world, and her husband was about to call off the wedding because of it. But again, God interceded and sent an angel to keep Joseph from hijacking His plan.

Now, consider the weight of all the whispers and understandable accusations. The angel didn't visit everyone in their family and community and fill them in on God's plan. And the more you try to convince someone that you talk to angels, the crazier you sound. Mary and Joseph had to move up their wedding date. The typical weeklong feasts and fanfare were cut back. To those unaware of God's plan, their wedding felt more like a funeral. This was not what they had dreamed of. This was far more than they could have ever imagined.

As if that wasn't enough, their intolerable isolation was broken by inconvenience. The ruler of the occupying power decided that it was time for a census. You know how a government loves its censuses! The census forced a very pregnant Mary and her husband to travel back to his family's hometown of Bethlehem. This was roughly an

80-mile journey ... on a donkey ... nine months pregnant. When Jeanne was nine months pregnant, she couldn't even handle the five-minute ride to Chick-fil-A for a chocolate shake. Mary and Joseph took the better part of a week to travel 80 miles to a city where they had no reservations and no connections.

You are no doubt familiar with the story. There was nowhere for them to stay. Nowhere for them to go, 80 miles from their family and community that still questioned Mary's pregnancy. No matter how much we try to paint them as saints, you have to believe that this was a very trying and difficult moment for Mary and Joseph.

In a final act of desperation, Joseph talked someone into opening up their garage, pushing some of the mess aside, and letting them stay there. This stranger's garage would become the birthplace of the Savior of the world. No doctor, no doula, no comfort, no privacy. There was blood and screaming and cold and animals and dung and hay. And before Mary could even get her new baby to learn to latch, strangers came stumbling in. Shepherds: social outcasts who spent the majority of their days talking to animals.

This was the world that Jesus entered into. This is what God chose. It is hard to find a more obscure and insignificant birth than that of Jesus. I have been in Zambia, hours after babies were born to teenage mothers in the home where eight other family members were piled in. And even those moments had more dignity and comfort than the birth of Jesus.

It's almost as if God is letting you know that no matter how insignificant or low your life may seem or feel, Jesus has already been there. He started there. He entered into this world in the lowliest of ways so that He can meet you wherever life may have taken you.

The birth of Jesus is as miraculous as it is common. It is something of both heaven and earth. He would later talk about the kingdom of God—*the* way of heaven here on earth. His birth is our first picture of that: the human and divine in an inseparable swirl. God with Us. Us with God. Glory breaking through our boring story. The birth announcement of Jesus is an invitation to all people that life with God came at a great cost and is now freely available to all.

The gospel accounts, each in their own unique voice, tell us of the events and the impact of the birth of Jesus. Some give great detail, while others paint in broad strokes. But they all tell how everything changed the moment that God came to be WITH us. They speak of the immediate and eternal impact of His birth ... and then they say very little about how He grew up.

In-Between Days

The Christian faith hangs its hope on the birth, life, death, and resurrection of Jesus. These events and the implications they bring are the cornerstone of Christianity. The evidence of a God who came to be WITH us and offer His life for us. This is the truth that has changed my life. But what I find interesting is that 100 percent of what I believe about the birth, life, death, and resurrection of Jesus is really only based on 20 percent of the life He lived with us.

Jesus lived, here on earth, for somewhere in the ballpark of 33 years. The Bible gives us a great account of the last three years of His life. We know about His birth and have a rough idea of the first two years of His life. The gospel of Luke tells of Him and His family visiting the temple when He was 12 ... but that's it. From age two to 12 and from age 12 to 30, we simply don't know or have any account.

There's speculation. There are some great works of fiction about this time. But aside from that, we have very little to go on for roughly 80 percent of Jesus' life. In an era when we share every seemingly insignificant detail of our everyday lives as well as what we had for dinner with the entire world, it's hard to imagine *not* knowing the details of the majority of the life of the most important person in history.

We live in a day that demands details, in a world where the pursuit of reasonable proof often precedes real faith. However, I find that it is this mystery regarding the majority of Jesus' life that actually increases my faith. It intrigues me while at the same time encourages me. Could it be that while Jesus was with us, He had days just as uneventful as mine? Could it be that He had chores, and eventually work, and awkward relatives, and long dull days, and jokes that weren't as funny as He thought they would be? Could it be that in many ways His unrecorded life was a lot like mine? Could it be that not every day was filled with miracles and great movements of God? That water stayed water, the sick stayed sick, and the dead stayed dead? That the "then and there" of the cross was a lifetime away from the "here and now" of His everyday life?

Could it be that all those years that we know nothing about were nothing less than an underline to the word WITH? Jesus' commitment was to be with us, even when no one was writing anything down or even thinking that they should. He chose to be with us in our everyday joy and pain, our loves and losses, our work and play, our most meaningful and forgettable moments.

Maybe that is what it means for Him to be 100 percent WITH us. Jesus was willing to be 100 percent present even when the cameras were off. The first 30 years of His life matter as much as the last three. And even though all we'd ever hear about was 20 percent of His life, it's not hard to imagine a Savior who was ... and is ... 100 percent with us, even in the midst of our boring everyday lives.

What Life with God Looks Like (Matthew, Mark, Luke, John)

Everything Jesus did while on earth becomes clearer through the lens of WITH. From His teaching, to His miracles, to the people He surrounded Himself with, to the way He prayed—the life of Jesus is what a life *with* God looks like. The more you explore the life of Jesus, the more you begin to understand the lengths to which God went to be WITH us and the depths of His love made evident to us in Him.

The Teachings of Jesus—How to Live WITH God

On a recent flight back to Chicago, it dawned on me that I have learned to ignore just about *everything* the flight attendants share during the preflight safety instructions. We all know this information is important. We all know it's true. We all know that it comes from people smarter than we are. It's information that can literally save our lives, but we do whatever we have to do to not have to hear it—from thumbing through the *Sky Mall* catalog and seriously considering the purchase of an authentic Elven Sword from *Lord of the Rings*, to sneaking a headphone into your non-exposed ear, to faking that you're asleep ... to actually being asleep. People are sharing life-saving information with me, and I simply ... don't ... hear it.

So it often is with the teachings of Jesus. Maybe you grew up hearing it. Or you've read the bumper stickers and seen the T-shirts. You hear it in church over the weekend. And maybe you feel encouraged, or challenged, or even convicted, ... but then ... like so much preflight information, it gets lost in the demands and distractions of everyday life. It's not because you're a bad person, it's just that what Jesus said about life with God can be really challenging or really confusing or really cost you something. And without the bigger context of what Jesus' teaching was pointing to, it's easy to get lost or overwhelmed and even discouraged.

The teachings of Jesus are far more than tweetable quotes or spiritual sound bites. They are the definitive declaration of a new way of living WITH God. Everything He taught was about what life with God really looks like. They illustrate how a loving God has been persistently pursuing you your entire existence and has created you for so much more than the life you may have settled for.

Jesus was a masterful teacher, unparalleled in His ability to communicate deep theological truth in unprecedented simplicity. Jesus knew exactly when to teach, when to ask questions, when to tell stories, and when to leverage moments that revealed what this life with God is really like.

I've always loved how Fredrick Buechner describes the teaching styles of Jesus: He says that,

> He suggests rather than spells out. He evokes rather than explains. He catches by surprise. He doesn't let the homiletic seam show. He is sometimes cryptic, sometimes obscure, sometimes irreverent, always provocative.[1]

There is *far* too much of Jesus' teaching for us to cover in one chapter. But I believe that camping out on a few key moments of teaching from Jesus will help you see the greater picture of what underlines all of Jesus' teaching—what life *with* God looks like.

Consider the first recorded teaching that we have of Jesus—in Luke 4: His ten-minute sermon in the temple in His hometown of Nazareth. It caused a riot to break out and propelled Jesus into His public teaching ministry.

Now, I remember the first sermon I ever gave. I was 14. It was to a Sunday school room of squirmy little three-to-four year olds. They

---

1. Frederick Buechner, *Telling the Truth: The Gospel as Tragedy, Comedy, and Fairy Tale* (New York: Harper & Row, 1977), 63.

were hopped up on graham crackers and paper shot glasses of water. A very captive audience! I taught about Jesus and the moment when some guys lowered their paralyzed friend through a hole in the roof to get to Jesus. I even built a shoebox diorama, with G.I. Joe figures and all! I realize now that it must have been hard for a four year old to accept Jesus' teaching to "Turn the other cheek" when a G.I. Joe Jesus is holding an AK–47 and strapped with grenades . . . and comes riding into Jerusalem on an ATV. Nevertheless, my first sermon went off without a hitch and began a lifelong calling to communicate the love of God by using my God-given voice.

Now imagine that you are Jesus (the real one . . . not the G.I. Joe one), and you are about to give your first sermon. What would *you* teach? What would you want to lead off with? Heaven and hell? Sin? Marriage? The importance of reading your Bible? Jesus' choice is fascinating, and not surprisingly, it's all about who God is for and who God is WITH.

It's found in Luke 4:16–21. Jesus has just been baptized. He had spent forty days in the desert fasting and being tempted by Satan himself. He's in His hometown of Nazareth. Mary is there. She has made signs and banners for everyone. Jesus goes to the temple, the one He grew up learning and worshiping in. It's a hometown crowd . . . and this is what Jesus says. He opens the scroll to the text of Isaiah 61 and reads,

> "The Spirit of the Lord is on me,
>   because he has anointed me
>   to proclaim good news to the poor.
> He has sent me to proclaim freedom for the prisoners
>   and recovery of sight for the blind,
> to set the oppressed free,
>   to proclaim the year of the Lord's favor."

Jesus rolls up the scroll and sits down. Everyone's eyes are fixed on Him. Then he says,

> "Today this scripture is fulfilled in your hearing." (Luke 4:21)

This was Jesus' inaugural sermon. In essence, He was saying, "I have come to be *with* those whom no one else wants to be with. I am not only *with* you, I am *for* you. You, whom society has forsaken, the Father has not forgotten. He is with you. And you can be with Him!"

The crowd was impressed. They liked the sentiment, but this wasn't what they came for. They came for a show! They wanted Him to perform miracles. They expected Jesus to give them special treatment because they used to live down the street from Him. Their expectations of Jesus quickly turned into demands, as ours so often do. So He told them "no." He refused to play by their expectations for preferential treatments and fair-weathered faith. He would not do any "tricks" for them on this day or any day … and this was their response:

> All the people in the synagogue were furious when they heard this. They got up, drove him out of the town, and took him to the brow of the hill on which the town was built, in order to throw him off the cliff. But he walked right through the crowd and went on his way. (Luke 4:28–30)

They tried to *kill* Jesus! After His *first* message! That's quite a response! So if you're ever discouraged after a bad presentation at work, a failed pickup line, or a bad interview, be encouraged by this: At least no one is trying to kill you over it!

In His first recorded sermon, Jesus talked about people—people He came to be with. He could have spoken about a lot of hotbed issues of the day. There are a lot of *what's* that Jesus could have taught about,… but instead He focused on *who*. He declared right off the bat that He came to be WITH.

This was always at the heart of Jesus' teaching—who God is and what life *with* Him is like. Each new teaching was erasing the old lines drawn by religious elitists and opening the invitation to relationship with God to all who recognized their need for Him. This invitation to life *with* God is illustrated through what is perhaps the most recognizable and familiar teaching of Jesus, the Sermon on the Mount, found in Matthew 5.

Look at *who* Jesus declares that God is WITH:

"Blessed are the poor in spirit,
  for theirs is the kingdom of heaven.
Blessed are those who mourn,
  for they will be comforted.
Blessed are the meek,
  for they will inherit the earth.
Blessed are those who hunger and thirst for righteousness,
  for they will be filled.
Blessed are the merciful,
  for they will be shown mercy.
Blessed are the pure in heart,
  for they will see God.
Blessed are the peacemakers,
  for they will be called children of God.
Blessed are those who are persecuted because of righteousness,
  for theirs is the kingdom of heaven."

"Blessed are you when people insult you, persecute you and falsely say all kinds of evil against you because of me. Rejoice and be glad, because great is your reward in heaven, for in the same way they persecuted the prophets who were before you." (Matt. 5:3–12)

The message of Jesus is good news for those who know they're not good enough, for those who know that they need God, for those who have lost faith in themselves and found it in God. Imagine seeing Him that day, hearing Him teach … and knowing that He is talking to you. That the God of the Universe sees you—and not only sees you, but is with you. And not only with you, but has moved heaven and earth to be with you. That's a pretty powerful thing to consider.

The message of how to live life with God comes through not only Jesus' sermons, but also the parables that He taught. The parables of the Lost Sheep, the Lost Coin, and the Lost Son (Luke 15) all illustrate the lengths to which God goes to be with us. The parable of the Wedding Banquet (Matt. 22:1–14) paints a picture of God's heart for the lowly, looked over, and looked down upon. The parable of the Merciful Servant (Matt. 18:21–35) shows how we are to live with one another in the presence of the forgiveness of Jesus. And that's just to name a few parables.

This is what we see throughout the teachings of Jesus. Whether it's sermons or parables or teachable moments Jesus was ever reiterating who God is and that He has come to have relationship with us. He taught that there is a new way of living in this world WITH Him. His teaching is equal parts illustration, explanation, and invitation to a life WITH God. They consistently point to another way—an upside-down way that is *actually* the way things are meant to be.

Where grace and growth are inseparable.

Where forgiveness flows freely and frees fully.

Where we strive to serve instead of seeking to be served.

Where the poor and oppressed and overlooked are protected and provided for.

Where the dark draw of sin is eclipsed by the bright light of God's love.

Where the endless ladders of religion are obliterated, and bridges are built to those who previously assumed that their separation from God was a permanent condition.

Jesus' teaching still holds. His truth still transforms. And His invitation still stands: "Come to Me, ... be with Me. All you who are weary and beat up by this life. Who have lost faith in religion. Who've lost faith in yourself. Find it in Me. And as you do, you will find rest, and peace, and purpose for your soul."

The Miracles of Jesus:
God Is WITH the Powerless and Faithful

Few things in the life of Jesus have drawn more attention and raised more debate than His miracles. To some, they are all the proof needed to accept the divinity of Jesus. To others, they are the fairy-tale straw that breaks the historical back of Jesus and makes Him too difficult to believe. I believe that they are much more. The miracles of Jesus are yet another way that God demonstrates that He is WITH those who are powerless, but full of faith. They are a small pulling back of the curtain between heaven and earth. They are the alchemy of divinity meeting humanity. They are as purposeful as they are powerful, and they always reveal the heart of a God who is not only *with* us ... but *for* us.

What is interesting about the miracles of Jesus is how such great power can be focused often times on such small things. Turning water into wine. Healing a sick child. Restoring physical wholeness and human dignity to a handful of blind folks, people who are crippled, and those with leprosy. Feeding a crowd of 5,000 in one moment—okay, that's a big one! Jesus started that miracle with a small sack lunch. Each miracle is a small display of Jesus' great power to meet specific needs. In what could easily be seen as "showboating," Jesus shows us how much God is *with* us, by *whom* and *what* these miracles were performed for.

Have you ever personally prayed for some kind of miracle? Either for help with something that seemed utterly impossible by human odds? Or for healing for someone who was sick or dying? Or for the highway patrol officer to be in an inexplicably good mood and decide to let you off with a warning? We all have. You have no doubt thrown your own Hail Mary prayers to God—those long-shot, act-of-God kinds of prayers that we offer as our last-ditch desperate attempt to get God to move. The truth is, you wouldn't throw those types of prayers out there if you didn't believe at some level that God could do something. You believed enough to ask Him for a miracle. It was this kind of small but honest faith that compelled Jesus to release God's power into the lives of ordinary everyday people He healed and blessed. Jesus was moved by their faith.

I remember the first time that I saw the street magician, performance artist, and levitating human ice cube David Blaine. I came across a late-night magic infomercial that he made by himself, with special celebrity host Leonardo DiCaprio (which is perhaps Blaine's greatest trick to date). I vividly remember throwing down the remote control in shock over the kinds of tricks that he performed and then subsequently not sleeping well that night. I had never seen anything like that. It was rather disorienting to see someone do something that is seemingly impossible.

The only problem with folks like David Blaine is that once they do the seemingly impossible, they have to do it again ... and again ... and again. The job description of magicians is to outdo themselves. To do it bigger and better than anyone ever before, including themselves. To work harder and harder at keeping people's attention while keeping them distracted.

This was not the case with the miracles of Jesus. His miracles were not grandstanding demonstrations of the awe and power of God. They were revelations of God's glory to meet a very small human need. They were often intimate. In fact, several times Jesus tells those whom He has healed not to not mention it to anyone. Such is the case with the very first miracle of Jesus—the turning of water into wine.

This miracle took place at a wedding. Jesus was apparently His mother Mary's "Plus One," and yet somehow the disciples (who hadn't been with Jesus that long) managed to sneak in. The party was in full swing! The deejay had just finished playing "Celebrate" by Kool and the Gang. Everyone was busy dancing and drinking ... until the wine ran out!

> The wine supply ran out during the festivities, so Jesus' mother told him, "They have no more wine."
>
> "Dear woman, that's not our problem," Jesus replied. "My time has not yet come."...
>
> This miraculous sign at Cana in Galilee was the first time Jesus revealed his glory. And his disciples believed in him. (John 2:3–4, 11 NLT)

Here again we see Jesus revealing the great power of God to meet a very small human need. Did Jesus need to turn water into wine? Did thousands of people come forward to believe in Him after this miracle? No. In fact, hardly anyone even noticed. Just the caterers and the handful of disciples Jesus had called.

With many of Jesus' miracles, that wasn't even the point. Jesus didn't do miracles *so* that people would believe; He did miracles *because* people believed. Just about every one of the healing miracles that Jesus performed was preempted by the faith of the person whom Jesus was WITH. Even in that first miracle, we see that Mary came to Jesus because she believed that He could do something to keep that party from being a bust.

Whether it was a leprous outcast, a blind homeless man, a woman who had suffered from internal bleeding her entire life, or a desperate father who was losing his daughter, no matter who they were, it was their faith in Him that healed them. It was their belief that they were *with* someone who had the power to meet their needs, to heal their brokenness, to do the impossible. Not fully knowing if He would, but fully believing that He could.

This kind of faith is born out of dead ends; it rises from ashes and alleyways. And it is precisely the kind of faith that Jesus invites you to have in Him. This is, of course, much easier said than done, because the truth of my faith, and quite possibly yours, is that it is fluctuating at best, ever riding the currents of circumstances.

Your faith may seem small, but the good news is that if it's sincere, it's something Jesus can work with. He is quite familiar with fledgling faith. He had to deal with Peter for Pete's sake (which, I believe, is where that phrase comes from)! Jesus regularly and masterfully navigated the struggling doubts of religious people as well as the surprising faith of irreligious people. In fact, it is Jesus who is famously quoted for saying about faith,

> Truly I tell you, if you have faith as small as a mustard seed, you can say to this mountain, 'Move from here to there,' and it will move. Nothing will be impossible for you." (Matt. 17:20)

Your small faith in a great God can accomplish big things. This is what the miracles of Jesus teach us—that God wants to work not only *through* us, but *with* us. He makes much out of our minor faith. He proves that an ounce of faith in God weighs more than 200 tons of faith in ourselves. When you choose to live your everyday life *with* Jesus, your small faith becomes a conduit for the impossible. God does a lot with your little. And perhaps the greatest miracle of all is that when you give God your little faith … no matter how small it may seem … He grows it. He takes the little faith you give to Him and miraculously gives you more.

With even the smallest amount of faith to work with, I have seen God move mountains of resistance in my friends' lives. I have seen Him erode mountains of fear in my own life. I have seen Him move seemingly impassable and impenetrable mountains of people's pasts. With my own little faith, I have seen God move mountains of comfort and complacency that had compiled over the years. And in the space of that newly renovated real estate, where mountains had once blocked my view, exists a new horizon of faith and life *with* God!

You may feel that you have very little faith, no bigger than a mustard seed, but according to Jesus, that is exactly all He needs to work a miracle.

The Friends of Jesus—How to Live WITH God

They say that you can learn a lot about someone by the company they keep. Seeing the people you surround yourself with says something about the kind of person you are. Who you are *with* greatly shapes and forms who you are.

So, to better understand who Jesus is and the kind of relationship He offers you, it would make sense to look to the people whom He was in relationship with. The disciples of Jesus serve as one of our greatest glimpses into a God who is WITH us. In fact, the choice and empowerment of His disciples is what sets Jesus apart from every other significant major religious leader. It's not just *that* He had disciples, but more importantly, *whom* He had as disciples. Not a single disciple was chosen because of world-changing qualifications. They were not chosen because they were the brightest and best of their day. They were not chosen merely to be Jesus' followers; they were invited to be His friends. They were the people *with* whom Jesus shared His life—the people He shared meals with, shared tears with, shared joy with, shared pain with. His choice of them said as much about *Him* as it did *them*.

I remember the first real work team that I was invited to be a part of. It was the staff team in the high school ministry of Willow Creek Community Church in Illinois. I loved being a part of that team. All of us were young and unproven leaders. We were full of dreams and vision and the confidence that comes with being in your mid-twenties. We genuinely loved one another. We were deeply competitive with each other. (There were more than a few Monopoly games that ended with team members not speaking to each other for a day or two.) We were committed to each other, pushed each other, carried each other, and when needed, forgave each other. Beyond all of that, we were deeply believed in by our boss, Bo. He was a coach in every sense of the word. In fact, on more than one occasion when he wanted to make a point or mark a moment, he would have us huddle around him and take a knee (true story). None of us believed that we deserved to be there ... and yet all of us were invited. It was a truly great team.

If there was a common denominator that our team was built on it was simply this: *willingness*. There was a shared spirit of willingness to do whatever it took to accomplish the vision God had given us. There was a willingness on our leaders' part to believe in us (despite some better judgment). There was a willingness to take big risks and go out on a limb for God. While it may not seem like much on the surface, willingness is a force to be reckoned with. It is the cauldron where courage and resolve are forged. Beyond wishing ... beyond wanting ... there is willing.

While there must have been many more qualified leaders for Jesus to choose from, his disciples did have something in common. Something that Jesus saw. Something deep within them that they might have never noticed, but that Jesus recognized right away: they were *willing*. When Jesus said the words, "Come. Follow me. Do life with me. Leave that numb and comfortable life behind and be my disciple," they were willing. They said yes. And with the exception of Judas, they continued to say yes to Jesus right up to their last breath.

Jesus made a choice. He could have very easily come as a Solo Savior, an Independent Contractor sent here to save this world from itself ... all by Himself. But he chose to be *with* the most unsuspecting, long-shot, last-to-be-picked folks imaginable. Just look at His "With List":

Peter (Simon) and Andrew	Passionate first followers
James and John	The Sons of Thunder
Philip	Faithful
Bartholomew	Good with knots
Matthew	Good with money
Judas	Too good with money
Thomas	Honest
James	Great with directions
Simon	The other Simon
Thaddeus (aka Jude)	The hypeman
Mary, Martha, and Lazarus	Home away from home

There was not a religious leader in the bunch, nor were there any well-connected politicians or influencers among them. Not one of them was famous (at least not when they knew Jesus). There was nothing special about a single one of them ... except for what Jesus saw in them. He knew that time spent with Him would change them. He knew that, just like you and me, they would be shaped by the *Who* they were *with*.

Each of us, whether we realize it or not, has a With List. They are people whom, for this reason or that (or sometimes, for no good reason at all), we have chosen to live this life with. Who are those people for you? Who makes it onto your With List?

I have created some space below to help you with your With List.

Use the space on the left to write down the names of all the people you share your life with. They are the friends that you've invited into the truth of who you are. (For the sake of the exercise, spouses and family don't count.) When you have finished, how many folks made it onto the list? Any surprises? What does the number of people on that list tell you about the way you are doing life *with* others?

Now, for the space on the right, see if you can come up with a couple of adjectives to describe your relationship or the kind of life you live because of these relationships. In other words, who are *you* because of who *they* are?

Who	Because

My list would look something like this (in no particular order):

Marc	Honest sharpener
Josh	Thick and thin
Jon	Soulful and fun
Jeanne (not my wife)	Deep fun friend
Trent	Me 15 years younger

It's a powerful thing to step back and reflect on the "who's" that we are with and who we are becoming by being with them. Our lives are undeniably and indelibly marked by others. That is why it is so important that we actually have others in our lives who are helping us become who we are created by God to be and that we are in turn doing the same for them.

This is why the disciples are the perfect picture of a God who came to be WITH. A God who dives into the depths and dirt of our humanity, not to pull us out of it, but to be with us in it. He is a God who sees in us what can only be true of us through Him being with us. The invitation that He gave to every disciple has not changed: "Follow Me. Live your life with Me and discover what life is meant to be." The invitation still stands. You can actually live your life with the One who chose to live His life with us.

A God Who Is WITH Us Until the End

The death and ultimate resurrection of Jesus demonstrates the lengths to which God goes to be WITH us and for us. From the Last Supper until Jesus is buried in a borrowed tomb, He is never once truly alone. People are in His periphery right up to the end.

The Last Supper

First, there's the Last Supper, where Jesus gathers His followers together for what will be the last time that all 13 of them are together. There at the table, surrounded by the people whom He has chosen to do life with, Jesus declares that this very beloved community will betray Him and deny Him before the night is through. Even the community that Jesus chose to live His life with isn't perfect. It's just as broken as ours. Yet He is still present—living in the risk and rejection, the betrayal and denial that comes with community.

Knowing what was to come, Jesus still chose to be *with*, even as bread broke, and bonds broke, and the crumbs of community fell quietly on the table.

At the end of the meal, they spent time singing a worship song together (Matt. 26:30). Think about that. Can you fathom trying to sing with someone who sold you out ... or someone you knew was going to hurt you or betray you? I can't imagine it would be easy to nail those four-part harmonies together. I'd want to break out into James Brown's "The Payback" just to let them all know that I knew what was going on: *"I don't know karate, but I know ka-razy!"*

Even so, Jesus was *with*. He was with those whom He could have easily accomplished His mission without. Looking in each of their eyes ... one last time ... before they would have to look away from the brutality of His beatings and the cold conclusion of the cross.

The Garden

In the garden of Gethsemane, Jesus demonstrates His humanity and His need by asking His community to stay with Him as He entered into His Dark Night of the Soul.

> Then he said to them, "My soul is overwhelmed with sorrow to the point of death.
> Stay here and keep watch with me." (Matt. 26:38)

Yet again, His community failed Him. The Son of God was in need ... and they fell asleep. Have you ever found yourself in that place of desperate need when all you want is for someone to just ... be with you? Have you ever reached out to someone from that place, only to have them be a "no-show" in your time of need? If so, then you are closer to Jesus than you realize. Here we see the fragility of Jesus' humanity. He didn't choose to be with His disciples for their sake; He *needed* His disciples to be with Him for His sake. But they chose to close their eyes and sleep rather than see the need of their leader. So Jesus pressed on and stepped a few yards away from them to pray on His own. This was the closest He would be to being by Himself in those final hours.

This moment with Jesus in the garden has always been one of the hardest for me to swallow. While I do not believe that Jesus in this moment was doubting God, I do believe that He was desperate. A desperation that you feel like an ache in the guts of your faith. A desperation that calls into question the very character of God and is repelled by cheap and easy answers to the questions that keep us up at night.

There is, in the beginning of a life with Jesus, a seemingly effortless momentum that comes like a rising swell from deep within the vast ocean of faith, propelling us forward with exhilarating and sometimes terrifying delight. There is nothing like it. But like all waves, that "new season" eventually ... inevitably ... comes to an end. Sometimes it is a calm washing onto the old familiar shores of life. Other times the wave comes crashing down, leaving us disoriented and even defeated.

I know of several significant times when I hit the wall with God, and then the faith that once came so quickly and easily became hard to find and slow to arrive. I have spent seasons of waiting and wading in the water, wondering if I would ever feel Jesus with me the way I once did. Perhaps you have wondered and felt the same. Perhaps you're in that season now. You are not alone.

I am reminded of Agnes, a woman familiar with the desperation Jesus faced in the garden. For as long as Agnes could remember, she had loved God. As she grew older, her faith grew stronger, leading her to become a full-time missionary at a relatively young age. Her faith and faithfulness bore great fruit. Within a few short years of being a missionary, she was leading a thriving ministry. Her organization was serving thousands of poor and sick and dying people. Eventually the eyes of the world fell upon this five-foot-tall giant of faith. In a season when her ministry was at its greatest reach and when the world regarded her as a saint, she wrote these desperate words in her journal,

> "Where is my faith? Even deep down there is nothing but emptiness and darkness.
> My God, how painful is this unknown pain ... I have no faith."

Her close friends had known of her desperate struggle for faith. They wondered if she would ever come out of this deep dark cave of doubt. They prayed for her daily. And when they prayed for her, they prayed for her by name. They knew her as Agnes ... but the world would remember her as Mother Teresa.

All of the following great leaders of the faith wrote about their struggle with faith and doubt and seasons when they wondered if Jesus was really *with* them anymore.

Mother Teresa	Dietrich Bonhoeffer
Billy Graham	Saint John of the Cross
Henri Nouwen	King David
C.S. Lewis	

For some of us, the struggle comes in college. All the faith of childhood gets packed up in a box to take away to school, only to find that it doesn't fit anymore, so back in the box it goes.

For others, the wondering of the presence of Jesus comes when a deeply personal and significant prayer is seemingly unanswered by God. Or answered in a way that doesn't fit the picture and timeline imagined. It could be a prayer for healing in your life or the life of someone you love. It could be a one-year ... two-year ... three-year long prayer for a job — or the heartfelt or heartbroken prayer for someone to spend your life with, or the prayer for a baby or a wayward child. Pray any prayer long enough with no clear results that meet with your hopes, desires, or expectations ... and your faith begins to wane and waver. You will wonder what WITH really means.

When you don't "feel" that you have much faith left or when you wonder if Jesus really *is* with you, it's easy to assume that the opposite of faith is *doubt* and that if you don't "feel" the faith you once felt, then doubt is your only option. You conclude that you either believe or you don't, that if it doesn't seem as though Jesus is with you ... then He isn't. That it's either one or the other.

But the soul God gave you is far more complex than that. It is a vast ocean big enough to handle the ebb and flow of faith and doubt. You are a dynamic individual created by God with a powerful and mysterious soul that is filled with both ... sometimes at the same time. One does not cancel the other out. In fact, faith and doubt are better friends than you might have imagined.

Doubt is a sort of check engine light for your soul, the sign of a faith that's ready to grow up. Doubt says, "There's more here," and "Don't settle," and "It's time to grow up." Doubt says, "Let's paddle out farther." It is actually the evidence that your faith is dynamic, that it is growing, or at the very least, that it needs to grow. Jesus is with you in your doubt *and* is waiting for you out past these waves. Even when you wonder if He's with you, you are not alone. You are surrounded by a sea of people of great and little faith — people whose faith has been shaped by their doubts.

To walk *with* Jesus means that you walk with Him to the Garden of Despair. It means that, at times, you walk hand in hand with doubt. You walk with questions. You walk with wondering. And yet somehow, even in the darkest hours, when the world you know has fallen asleep around you ... you know that He walks WITH you ... through it all ... and that He will never walk away.

The Trial

Jesus was arrested in the garden of Gethsemane, and the long night of false accusations and false trials began. His disciples awoke from their sleep into a nightmare. It was all happening, exactly as Jesus said it would—including the part where they would betray and deny and abandon Him. The absence of His followers was replaced by the presence of His accusers. All night they were with Him, squeezing Him in and out of the cracks of the legal system.

Eventually, their intricate and elaborate plan worked. Jesus was ultimately sent to the cross by Pontius Pilate, the highest-ranking local Roman official. Jesus was beaten, mocked, and ridiculed—this on top of the betrayal and abandonment from his closest friends. He was given His cross and sent marching to Golgotha ... and once again ... He was not alone.

The Cross

Even as He hung on the cross ... He was WITH. Jesus was flanked by two criminals, to His left and right. Just as in life, even in death, Jesus is *with*.

The Bible says in Matthew 27:44 that both of the thieves spent some of their last words cursing Jesus, blaming Him for their condition. "If you are the Son of God, then do something about it! Get us out of here. Save us, and we'll follow you!" Jesus offered no response. But the Bible implies that something changed in the hearts of one of those thieves. Despite all the horrible things he had seen in his life, he began to see something different in Jesus. It was something he had been secretly searching for all of his life. There was life in that dying body of Jesus—life unlike anything he had ever experienced. Something began to change. He called out to the other criminal, "What are you doing? Can't you see, he really is the Son of God? And they're killing him! We're here because we deserve to die. But he's done nothing wrong."

"Jesus," the thief cried out. "Remember me when you come into your kingdom!"

Jesus turned His attention to the dying criminal, now full of faith, and mustered up these last few words: "My friend I will. Tonight you will be *with* me in paradise." Even in death ... even in life after death, Jesus is *with* us. His invitation to life with Him means partaking in His death with Him so that we can experience real life with Him. His invitation to that criminal in the midst of His final breaths is the same invitation He extends to you, whatever condition your life may be in. You can have life with Jesus, both now and forevermore. On earth and in heaven. You can choose to live your life with the One who surrounded His life with people He loved until the very end of His life.

The Resurrection of Jesus

It is interesting to see who was WITH Jesus even in His death. Who are those who *stayed* with Him? Who are those who were *drawn* to Him ... even amid His capital punishment? It is in the response of those gathered there at the cross that we can find our own response to a Savior who would not only humble Himself but humiliate Himself by submitting Himself to death, especially death on a cross. Look at the varied responses in the very moment of the death of Jesus:

> And when all the crowd that came to see the crucifixion saw what had happened, they went home in deep sorrow. But Jesus' friends, including the women who had followed him from Galilee, stood at a distance watching. (Luke 23:48–49 NLT)

Look at the *crowds* who were with Jesus in His death. These are the same people who hailed Jesus as king only days before, and now they have gone back to their homes. They have gone to finish the Passover celebration and begin their day of Sabbath. Ken Gire points out how amazing it is that they could so savagely crucify Jesus and yet so solemnly honor their religious tradition.[2] Can you imagine being a part of something so horrific and then putting on your Sunday-best clothes and worshiping God?

How about the *disciples*? Where are they? Well ... they have gone into hiding. Peter has betrayed Jesus. Judas has killed himself. The rest of the disciples are hiding out behind locked doors in fear for their lives. In Jesus' greatest hour of need, in the darkest hour in human history, they are nowhere to be found.

All that remains at the cross is a *fractured handful of fatigued followers* — the Marys, John the beloved, and a few others. In fact, the Bible names two followers who had up to this point kept their allegiance to Jesus a secret: Joseph and Nicodemus. But something happens to them at the cross that forces a response.

> Now there was a good and righteous man named Joseph. He was a member of the Jewish high council, but he had not agreed with the decision and actions of the other religious leaders. He was from the town of Arimathea in Judea, and he had been waiting for the Kingdom of God to come. (Luke 23:50–51 NLT)

Joseph of Arimathea was a very wealthy man who was a part of the religious leaders who called for Jesus' death only hours before. This secret disciple of Jesus had been waiting for the kingdom of God to come. In the shadow of the cross he saw that kingdom. And he was about to do something that could cost him everything

> [Joseph] went to Pilate and asked for Jesus' body. Then he took the body down from the cross and wrapped it in a long sheet of linen cloth and laid it in a new tomb that had been carved out of rock. (Luke 23:52–53 NLT)

---

2. Ken Gire, *Moments with the Savior: A Devotional Life of Christ* (Grand Rapids: Zondervan, 1998), 373.

Joseph wanted to give Jesus a decent burial. So there in the shadow of the cross he decided to give to God his brand new garden tomb, one carved out of rock, one that had never been used. These were very expensive tombs. Tombs that were purchased and reserved for a wealthy family to use for generations. It most certainly cost him a fortune. It would also most likely cost him his career. And it could have cost him his life. But somehow the bruised and broken body of Jesus was still stirring life deep within people. People like Joseph and Nicodemus.

> He [Joseph] was accompanied by Nicodemus, the man who had earlier visited Jesus by night. Nicodemus brought a mixture of myrrh and aloes, about seventy-five pounds.... Since the tomb was nearby, they laid Jesus there. (John 19:39, 42)

So we have Joseph and Nicodemus burying the body of Jesus in a borrowed tomb. Therefore, much like His birth, we see Jesus once again without a place of His own to lay His head. I find it fascinating that the place where He was buried has been called the "Garden Tomb." How perfectly poetic! It was in a garden that sin entered our story, and it would be in a garden that it would be defeated once and for all. It was in a garden that the stage was set for BETWEEN. And it was in a garden that Jesus would set the stage for IN.

So here we see Jesus, like a seed being buried into the soil of a garden tomb, but this Seed will not stay in the ground for long. By God's power, Jesus will be brought from death to life, and the fruit of His resurrection will bring *life* to all who receive it.

For it is in *this* garden that we see that Joseph and Nicodemus were not alone. The women at the cross followed these two to the tomb and began to use Nicodemus's spices to prepare the body of Jesus for burial.

> Then they went home and prepared spices and ointments to anoint his body. But by the time they were finished the Sabbath had begun, so they rested as required by the law. (Luke 23:56 NLT)

Try and imagine that Passover. Imagine the silence. Imagine knowing that your hope lay locked away in a garden tomb, while you remained locked away in the prison of your home. But look at what happened:

> But very early on Sunday morning the women went to the tomb, taking the spices they had prepared. They found that the stone had been rolled away from the entrance. So they went in, but they didn't find the body of the Lord Jesus. (Luke 24:1–3 NLT)

The void left in the physical absence of Jesus was palpable. Imagine what it must have been like to be those first friends and followers of Jesus. To know that He had come to be WITH you ... but to now be *without* Him. To know what only a historical handful of people had known—the physical presence of God with them ... and then, to their seeming surprise ... not with them. Somehow they mustered on, going through the motions of grief.

John 20:11 begins an inside account as to how they began to move on without Jesus. Mary of Magdela had come to the tomb, but Jesus wasn't there! She freaked out, rightly so. She ran back to tell the disciples—the so-called "spiritual leaders," the few to whom Jesus had confided the most—but they didn't believe her. They thought she was crazy. John and Peter came to check it out, yet all they saw was an empty tomb and walked away troubled and confused. But then we see Mary. She couldn't leave. She couldn't believe that Jesus was gone. So she broke down and began to cry. Then ...

> Mary was standing outside the tomb crying, and as she wept, she stooped and looked in. She saw two white-robed angels, one sitting at the head and the other at the foot of the place where the body of Jesus had been lying. (John 20:11–12)

Mary was reminded of the descriptions of the ark of the covenant she had studied as a child. It, too, was adorned with two angels at each end, one at the head and one at the foot. But these angels weren't just architectural features; they were real and they asked,

> "Woman, why are you crying?"
>
> "They have taken my Lord away," she said, "and I don't know where they have put him." At this, she turned around and saw Jesus standing there, but she did not realize that it was Jesus.
>
> He asked her, "Woman, why are you crying? Who is it you are looking for?"
>
> Thinking he was the gardener, she said, "Sir, if you have carried him away, tell me where you have put him, and I will get him." (John 20:13–15)

You have to love how Mary was so desperate to find Jesus that she couldn't even see Him right in front of her. She literally thought He was the gardener! As if He rode up on a John Deere and was about to rake! How many times have I been searching for Jesus, looking for Him on my own terms and expectations, and have missed His loving presence right in front of me all along? Mary's eyes were opened the moment she heard her name.

> Jesus said to her, "Mary."
>
> She turned toward him and cried out in Aramaic, "Rabboni!" (which means "Teacher"). (John 20:16)

Here we see Jesus coming to be WITH Mary Magdalene. A woman. Someone whose testimony in that culture and at that time wouldn't even hold weight in court. He could have appeared in the temple or in the city square or to the disciples. But interestingly, He appears to someone who actually came looking for Him.

For most of my life I had assumed that the reason God rolled the stone away was so that Jesus could get out. Let's be honest: How terrible would it have been for Jesus to be resurrected by God, only to be stuck behind that rock, calling out, *"Hello?! Anyone out there? It's Me, Jesus, the Son of God! Risen from the dead! Can someone give Me a hand with this rock? I've kind of got a lot to do. I've got some appearances I need to make!"*

Is that why the stone was rolled away? Hardly. There's not a rock on this planet that could hold Him back. The tomb wasn't opened so He could get out, but so that you and I could go in. It was rolled away so that we could see that Death is defeated, that nothing can separate us from God: no rock, no temple curtain, no sin, no death, no fear! Nothing can separate you and me from the love of God found in the risen Jesus.

Mary went in and saw that Jesus had already come to her, so she ran from that empty tomb to tell everyone she knew that love wins, that hope prevails, that Jesus was alive!

> Mary Magdalene went to the disciples with the news: "I have seen the Lord!" (John 20:18)

I long to live with this kind of joy and confidence. I want to live with this kind of life — life that only comes from an empty tomb and a risen Jesus. The empty tomb of Jesus is a reminder to us that there is absolutely nothing that can keep us from God's extravagant love. Nothing!

This is why many years later, Paul could write with utter confidence,

> I am convinced that nothing can ever separate us from his love. Death can't, and life can't. The angels can't, and the demons can't. Our fears for today, our worries about tomorrow, and even the powers of hell can't keep God's love away.
>
> Whether we are high above the sky or in the deepest ocean, nothing in all creation will ever be able to separate us from the love of God that is revealed in Christ Jesus our Lord. (Rom. 8:38 – 39 my paraphrase)

The resurrection of Jesus is an invitation for us to enter in, to see for ourselves that death is an empty, hollow hole in the ground. There is no longer *anything* between us and God. That stone was the last remaining remnant of centuries of life in BETWEEN. The sin that had separated us from God was not only rolled out of the way, but obliterated once and for all. And all that is left for you and me to do is simply ... enter in.

How to Spend a Day WITH Jesus

It's one thing to talk about how Jesus chose to be with "them" ... then, but it's entirely another thing to think about what it might look like for Him to be with you ... today. What does it look like to get the life of Jesus off the pages of the Bible and into the ordinary everyday moments of your life?

Have you ever considered what it would be like to spend an entire day with Jesus? From start to finish and all points in-between? What would you do? Where would you go? How would you schedule it? Would you make it a part of your regular schedule if you could? In light of God moving heaven and earth so that Jesus could be WITH us, I have to ask myself: What am I *really* willing to do just to be with Him?

For some people, focused time with Jesus is a part of their spiritual rhythm. They schedule time out of each month or year to pull away from the day to day in order to have a day with Him. Many times this will look like a silent or solo spiritual retreat. For some it's going to a cabin; for others it means checking in to a monastery or spiritual retreat center.

I will never forget my first silent retreat. I was so excited to have a whole "Day With Jesus"—just Him and me. There was no phone, no Palm-Pilot (yes, it was that long ago), no one there I knew, and absolutely no talking. Up to that moment in my life, I don't think I had ever gone an entire day without talking. But I was up for the challenge. I figured if worst came to worst and I got desperate, I could just talk to myself. I went to a Jesuit retreat center near Chicago. The place looked as if it had been pulled from another era and preserved perfectly. I loved it. I was given my own room to use as a home base for my time with Jesus. The inventory for that room was as follows:

Army-issue twin bed = 1	Outlets = 2
Lamp = 2 (1 floor, 1 desk lamp)	TV = 0
Desk = 1	Wi-Fi = 0
Chair = 1	Phone = 0
Spiritual retreat amateur suffering from mild technology withdrawal = 1	

I set my bag in the corner and sat down on my army-issue twin bed to put a plan together for my Day with Jesus. I pulled my Bible and notebook out and promptly ... fell asleep. Apparently I had no idea how exhausted I was from the work of being a pastor. When I eventually awoke from my nap several hours later, I found myself significantly disoriented. I wasn't sure where I was or how I got there. What was this place? Had I been kidnapped? And if so, why were they holding me in such a religiously themed holding cell? I couldn't be sure.

When I finally put it all together, I looked at my schedule, only to see that I was about to miss "silent lunch." I only had a few minutes to get there. Nothing says "silent retreat" like frantically running across the serene surroundings of a monastery. I made it to the silent lunch by the sweat of my brow ... literally. Then I sat and ate in total silence. There's something so centering about sitting in a room full of people and not saying a word. I have tried implementing this spiritual practice with our kids at home ... but it hasn't quite taken off as I had hoped.

After the silent lunch I headed out to the garden for a prayer walk. This time started out perfectly. I walked slowly, intentionally, and prayerfully. It was beautiful ... until it started raining. And not just raining; this was a "biblical wrath of God" kind of rain. This was *not* a part of the plan. I came here to be with Jesus ... and it didn't feel like it was working!

Needless to say, my Day with Jesus did not turn out the way I had planned or imagined. While there were powerful and poignant moments, there were also a lot of moments in-between. Moments where not much happened. Ordinary moments where Jesus was still with me. Moments like my nap. Moments like standing under a portico in the pouring rain fifteen feet from where I thought I was supposed to be. Moments that are a lot like the moments of my ordinary everyday life.

These kinds of retreats have become a part of my yearly rhythm with God. I schedule them. I look forward to them. I cherish them. But they are not real life. They are retreats. So the question is, how do we actually move forward with Jesus in a more consistent and accessible way? How do we spend *every* day WITH Jesus?

In their brilliant book *An Ordinary Day with Jesus,* authors John Ortberg and Ruth Haley Barton lay out a *way* of spending our normal, ordinary days fully aware of the power and presence of Jesus. Through simple practices and interruptions, we make ourselves more aware of what God has made available to everyone who is in relationship with Him—the gift of His presence. The idea is as practical as it is spiritual.

Think about the hundred things you do in a day that are rhythms and routines for you—things you do to make your life work. From brushing your teeth, to the way you do breakfast, to the way you have to have your coffee, to the route you take to work or school, to the regularity with which you check your email, text, Facebook, and Instagram. Call them "The things you do to be you." You do them every day, so much so in fact that you don't even think twice about them. You are already awesome at them.

So, the question is, How do you do what you already do with the One who created you? How do you connect with Jesus and stay connected with Him throughout the day and throughout whatever you're doing and whomever you're with? How do you invite and involve Jesus into all that you do throughout the day so that the sum of your ordinary moments becomes an extraordinary life with Him? Think for a moment about your Ordinary Day tomorrow. How might you spend it with Jesus? Here are a couple of thoughts and practices that help and shape me:

Good Morning, God! Before email, before breakfast, before you talk to anyone, acknowledge the presence of Jesus in your day and invite Him into any of the details, fears, joys, or hopes that come to mind as you're thinking through your day

Worship Feast. Earlier this year I took a fast from anything and everything I was pumping through my headphones and car stereo and chose only to listen to worship music. No radio, no new indie band that already broke up before you heard about them, no podcasts, and no NPR. I immersed myself in nothing but worship music. The change in my spirit and perspective was palpable. It is a simple practice that you can do tomorrow that can keep you closely connected with Jesus.

Tiny Silent Retreat. If you have a commute, see that time as a gift. Use it to be quiet and still. No radio or headphones or phone calls. You can pray. Or you can just be still and know that God is ... God. It's always a good exercise to pay special attention to where thoughts go when you are silent and still. What do you find yourself meditating on? Whatever it is, bring it to Jesus; He'll know what to do with it. (Special note for those of you who carpool: You might want to find another time to be completely silent and disengaged. No need to offend Susan!)

Scheduled Surprises. One of the ways we practice the presence of Jesus at Soul City Church is that from time to time we will set alarms in our phones or calendars to go off at random or intentional moments in the day with a one word or simple phrase prompt to pray. The intention is to stop whatever we're doing and spend a minute or two being present with God. Sometimes it will involve praying for a predetermined thing. Sometimes it will simply involve bringing wherever we're at and whatever we're doing and whatever we're feeling to God in that moment. I currently have the phrase "I'm Here" pop up every couple of hours in my day. It reminds me that wherever I'm at, whomever I'm with, whatever I'm doing ... God is there. He is with me. These little scheduled surprises serve as a kind of check-in, This is most powerful and effective when it's done in community. Knowing that there are others committed to connecting with God with you is a very inspiring and motivating thing.

Good Night, God! See "Good Morning, God!" ... only practice this one as the last thing you say or do at the end of your day. Let your last whisper of the day be into ear of the One who gave you that day and will sustain you through the night.

This is obviously a brief list. It barely scratches the surface of the possibilities and potential for you to be present with Jesus. There are more ways to do this. These are just a few that you can start right now. You don't have to schedule a silent retreat. You don't need to try to get everything perfect before you spend the day with Jesus. You don't even need to schedule it. You can begin today. You can practice the power of WITH by allowing Jesus to enter your world just as He entered our world some 2,000 years ago.

You can spend tomorrow's ordinary day with Jesus. Then you do the same the day after that ... and the one after that. When you continue to be with Him, your ordinary days with Jesus will transform to an extraordinary life with Him.

Conclusion: From WITH to IN

WITH is what the Gospels are all about. They are all about a God who came to be *with* us, so that He can do for us what we could never do for ourselves. He came to be *with* us to give His life *for* us so that we could live *with* Him. God is with us in our brightest, most uncontainable joys and in our darkest, most uncontrollable lows. God is with us in the outright extraordinary moments of life and in the downright ordinary moments as well. God is with us in our sin, in our confession, in our transformation, in our temptation, in our struggle, and in our victory. Jesus is God with us. But Jesus is not the end of the story of the Bible.

Jesus was acutely aware that His time on earth, like all things in this created world, was finite. It had an expiration date. He not only accepted it, but welcomed it. He talked about it, and He prepared His followers for it. Reflecting on the joyous fate set before Him, He said,

> "Very truly I tell you, unless a kernel of wheat falls to the ground and dies, it remains only a single seed. But if it dies, it produces many seeds." (John 12:24)

In this little metaphor, Jesus is predicting not only His death, but what is to come after it. As long as He remained in His physical form, there was only *one* of Him. God WITH us would be with only one person. As long as God was physically *with* us, He could only be *with* us in one place at one time. In a beautiful act of mutual submission, the deity of Jesus submitted to the physical limitations of the humanity of Jesus while the humanity of Jesus laid itself down so that the greater plan of God would prevail. The Son submits Himself to the greater work and timing of the Father, while the Spirit submits Himself to the greater work and timing of the Son. This is why Jesus knew that He needed to go, so that One could come who would redefine our old physical reality with a new spiritual reality.

Each movement in the story of God builds off of the previous one, lays a new foundation, and prepares us for what God is doing next. Each is what is needed at that time. The time of Jesus was perfectly timed in the greater story of God ... and then it was time for what was next. And what came next in the story of God is something that no one could have ever hoped for or imagined. While priests reminisced about how things used to be and prophets shot rocks across the rippling waters of a future they could not see, Jesus prepared His disciples for their new reality. He shared with His disciples in the final moments He had with them that the story was moving forward. God would be coming again, only in a different way ... a new way.

As we will see next, this was the Son preparing the way for the Spirit. This is how the story of God moves forward. This was the plan all along. This is God IN us.

4

Part Five

IN

Acts 2 to Revelation 22

The Big Idea of the Small Word: IN

The last word in the story of God is the word IN. God IN us. The God who has always been at the center of the story now enters IN to the story like never before by literally and spiritually entering IN to us. It completely shifts the story and shifts the way that we have relationship with God. This is what the story of God has been building to.

The same is true of your story and relationship with God.

- Your story has it's beginning in God. (*OF*)
- Your story with God has been a journey where at times there has been great distance. (*BETWEEN*)
- But God made a way for you to be in relationship with Him. (*WITH*)
- And He has offered you the invitation of this relationship with Him by entering into your life to love and lead and guide and guard every aspect of who you are. (*IN*)

IN was always the point. The relationship and proximity that was lost in the Garden was redeemed by something far greater. From intimacy with God to God IN me. To understand what this kind of relationship looks like and how you can actually experience it, we have to look to those who first experienced the glorious riches of this mystery—those first followers of Jesus and leaders of the first church. Through their lives, their experiences with God, and their writing and teaching about this new reality, we discover how we too can live this new life that God has for us IN Him ... with Him IN us.

Up to this point in the story, God had always been present, but still somehow distant. Present in the Garden, but separated by that thin, divine line of Creator and created. Present in covenants, commandments, priests, prophets, and kings, but separated by sin. Present in Jesus, like us in every way ... with the exception of His perfection. God was for the first time flesh and bone, but it would be these very limbs and ligaments that would be His limitation, because the power of His presence was confined by the contingency of proximity. The only way to be physically with Jesus was to be lucky enough to happen to be in the town that He was passing through, on the hill He happened to be teaching from, in a tree He happened to be walking by.

God has always been here, but the story forever changed once God came IN here. Once again, unlike any other deity, this God chose to do the unthinkable—to inhabit His people, to come *in* to our lives, to be all of who He is *in* all of who we are. No longer would God be somewhere out there or up there or over there or anywhere at a distance from us. No, this God came in, with an intimacy greater than the Garden, with a presence more powerful than promises, no longer limited to the location of one single solitary Jesus. No. This God is now present everywhere, in anyone who will say yes to Him. This was God's plan all along. This is the hope of glory. This is His hope for you—that you would experience the IN of God, the fullness of God, fully in you.

Starting a Church from Scratch

I have never experienced the power and possibility of a God who lives IN us more than I have over these past few years. Several years ago, my wife Jeanne and I found ourselves living a very comfortable life—a life we had worked hard to get to, but a life that required little of us and little of God. We had great jobs and a great church. We lived in a great house in a great neighborhood in Atlanta. Everything was ... great. But something wasn't well with our souls. We had a gnawing and nagging sense that God was inviting us into a life bigger than the one we had created for ourselves. Part of that life meant starting a church from scratch in Chicago.

This stirring quickly moved from weighing options to a question of "Will we obey?" So we did it. We cashed all our comfort in for courage. We forged our fear into faith and laid down control to pick up trust. It was the hardest and best thing we've ever done.

We realized very early in the process that this whole endeavor was much bigger than us and that it would require something of us that we were simply not capable of on our own. We had this sense that if we went about this great faith adventure by our own strength, we might be able to make it for a while, we might even get this thing off the ground and rolling ... but at what cost to our faith, to our marriage, to our family? We didn't want to be another church-planting casualty: People who gain a whole church but lose their own souls. We knew that we needed a faith and courage and wisdom and strength and perspective that simply could not come from ourselves. If this church was ever going to come out of us, then God would have to be IN us. So we determined to live out of our dependence on God. We decided that we would bank our lives on the promise of 1 John 4:4, which says, "the one who is *in* you is greater than the one who is in the world" (emphasis added).

Starting Soul City Church from scratch was one of the greatest opportunities for me to experience the reality of God's power and presence in my life. I just wish I hadn't waited so long to do it. I wish I wouldn't have waited so long, not just to start this church, but to start living out of a greater awareness of my inner dependence on God. I wish I wouldn't have waited for a "have to" situation to align my life around what was promised by Jesus all along.

I have lived the better part of my life aware that God is WITH me, but the same cannot be said of my awareness of God IN me. That is why I thank God for this chapter in the greater story. Acts 2 is the ever-reverberating firing of the starting gun to a new way of being in relationship with God. We can now be in relationship with God, but God being *in* us. IN changes everything!

How IN Entered In
(Acts 1–2)

IN begins at the end of WITH. Jesus had come. That's something worth truly considering—that, through Jesus, God had already come *down* before He ever came *in*. He lived His life with us, among us ... literally. Jesus immersed Himself in the sea of humanity being both fully God and fully us. He was crucified and raised by God from the dead, just as God had planned and promised.

His followers who had all but lost hope were reunited *with* Him again after His resurrection. You have to imagine that it all began to click for them, not in the way that Jesus had told and prepared them, but in their own presumptions of what would come next. How Jesus would overthrow their Roman oppressors. How Jesus would establish Himself as king just like all the prophecies seemed to say. How He would rule from David's throne with them right there by His side. Who would challenge Him? They had already killed Him, and He came back! This is it! Polish up the crowns and tiaras. Here we go! Like knights of the Lord's Table, the disciples were ready for the adventure that they thought was next ... only God had something better in mind.

Last Words

Although Jesus had spelled out all that would happen next, He felt the need to be explicit with them one last time. Acts 1:4 records:

> On one occasion, while he was eating with them, he gave them this command: "Do not leave Jerusalem, but wait for the gift my Father promised, which you have heard me speak about. For John baptized with water, but in a few days you will be baptized with the Holy Spirit."

Again, Jesus was being *very* specific with them. But they still didn't totally get it. Look at what Jesus said next:

> Then they gathered around him and asked him, "Lord, are you at this time going to restore the kingdom to Israel?"
> He said to them: "It is not for you to know the times or dates the Father has set by his own authority." (Acts 1:6–7)

Since they were *still* not getting it, Jesus decided to spell it out as clearly as possible. Just moments before He ascended into heaven, He said,

> "But you will receive power when the Holy Spirit comes on you; and you will be my witnesses in Jerusalem, and in all Judea and Samaria, and to the ends of the earth." (Acts 1:8)

That phrase "when the Holy Spirit comes on you" is what was new. This was the shift. God was coming not only into the world, but into us! And in the same way Jesus changed the world by entering into it, the Holy Spirit would change us by entering into us. According to Jesus, this next and new movement of the Spirit would give us a new power, a new purpose, and a new relationship with God.

Those are Jesus' final orders. "Stay here and wait for something to happen—something you've never experienced before, something that's never happened before in human history. Just stay here ... and wait. Everybody clear on the plan? Peter? I'm looking at you...."

Jesus planted the seed. The table was set. All was in place. But none of them could have predicted precisely what would come next. Jesus did an amazing job of telling them what the party was going to be like; He just hadn't told them exactly when it would start. All He told them to do was to wait, that they would know when it was time.

The Pentecost Festival

Jesus told the disciples to do their waiting in the city of Jerusalem, the religious capital of the world—which at best might have been confusing to His followers. You see, at the time, Jerusalem was celebrating what could be considered the Jewish World's Fair. Jews from all over the world had flocked to the city of Jerusalem for an annual religious festival that concluded with a celebration called "Pentecost."

For about two months out of the year, Jerusalem hosted a two-month-long sort of Mardi Gras ... only with a lot less drinking and mayhem and beads. Okay, it was nothing like Mardi Gras, but for two months Jewish pilgrims traveled from all over the known world to the city of Jerusalem to celebrate two key holidays: Passover and Pentecost.

Passover always held a special place in the life and rhythm of the people of God. It was a time to remember how God had delivered them from their oppressive captivity in Egypt. But this particular Passover was unique because this was the Passover when Jesus died on a cross and was raised by God from the dead. It didn't happen randomly. It happened on Passover weekend, in Jerusalem, a city that at that time had around 100,000 residents, but during the two months of Passover swelled to somewhere around 500,000 people! Some 400,000 tourists were present for that first Easter, and they were still there seven weeks later for Pentecost, a holiday that celebrates the first crop of the new season.

Jesus didn't give the disciples a whole lot more instruction than that they would know when it was time and He would tell them what to do. He did give them a promise, however, one that they could only understand once they had experienced it. He told them that in a matter of days, the Holy Spirit would come down to earth. And He wasn't coming just to visit, but to live ... forever. What's more, He would make His home IN the hearts of everyone who called Christ their Lord. And once again, Jesus told them to wait.

So that's what they did ... they waited—with all their excitement, all their hopes and dreams, confined to an upper-level flat in downtown Jerusalem. About 120 believers crammed in there, including Peter ... waiting. Not knowing what would come next. Not knowing that the hinge of history was swinging with every prayer they prayed, and not knowing that a revolution was brewing. But it was close, whatever it was. It was just a matter of time.

The Holy Spirit Arrives

Then it happened. At around 9 o'clock on the Sunday morning of Pentecost, the Holy Spirit shows up and bursts onto the scene. A wind breaks through that upper room and fills those gathered there. Without hesitation, they start worshiping. They are rocking out in the upper room, completely unaware that on the streets down below, people can hear them. Moreover, the people hear them worshiping in their own native tongues. These disciples are locals from Galilee, but all of a sudden they are worshiping God in Egyptian, Asian, Latin, and Greek.

A crowd begins to gather outside, and people want to know what in the world is going on. Some people think the disciples are just drunk. But Peter hops up and gives an excellent defense:

> Then Peter stood up with the Eleven, raised his voice and addressed the crowd: "Fellow Jews and all of you who live in Jerusalem, let me explain this to you; listen carefully to what I say. These people are not drunk, as you suppose. It's only nine in the morning!" (Acts 2:14–15)

Peter goes on to tell the huge crowd that was now flooding the street about who Jesus is and what His death and resurrection meant. Keep in mind that this is the same Peter who less than two months before denied that he even *knew* Jesus! This is Peter, the fisherman, the man who cut someone's ear off. Now he is giving one of the most powerful sermons in history. Finally, someone from the crowd interrupts him and asks the question that was on everyone's heart: "What must we do to know this Jesus?"

This Jesus—who only weeks earlier had to spell out the plan for His disciples—was now being proclaimed by those same disciples, and thousands of people were coming to faith in Him. In fact, more people decided to follow Jesus in the three months after His death than in the entire three years of His public ministry. Why? Aside from the power of the resurrection, I believe it was directly connected to the power of incarnation. God was no longer in human form; He was IN humans!

The day of Pentecost marks the first day and the first page of the chapter of IN. It marks a new era between God and us that Adam and Eve could have never conceived, that prophets could have only dreamed of, that Jesus knew all along:

> "I will not leave you as orphans; I will come to you. Before long, the world will not see me anymore, but you will see me. Because I live, you also will live. On that day you will realize that I am in my Father, and you are in me, and I am in you." (John 14:18–20)

Jesus knew that the same power that was His would be ours. Just as He was in God, God would be in us. We would be invited into the kind of relationship that Jesus had with His Father through the Holy Spirit. We would be invited to participate in the relational reality of the Trinity: knowing the Father, through the Son, by the Holy Spirit. The Holy Spirit is at the center of the story of IN. The little word ... that little preposition ... changed everything.

Can you remember the first prayer you ever prayed? Do you remember what it was about? The very first prayer I have on record was prayed as a young boy inviting Jesus IN to my heart. I always thought that was interesting language: "inviting Jesus into your heart." There is no account of anyone in the Bible "inviting Jesus into their heart." People invited Him into their homes, invited Him into theological debates and discussions, and invited Him to teach. Although there's not a single verse or a single mention of anyone "inviting Jesus into their heart," for many people who have come into a relationship with Jesus, this is the language they have used. We invite Jesus IN.

Not long after "inviting Jesus into my heart" I began to pray to God. My prayers were not complicated; they mostly had to do with thanking God for various meals and the hands that prepared them, asking Him to help me or others I knew to feel better, thanking Him for things that mattered to me, and asking for occasional traveling mercies (whatever those were). But before long, my prayers began to take on an interesting and all too common prepositional twist. I began to pray to a Jesus who was now somewhere "out there." I prayed to a God who was up in heaven and was far off.

Shortly after praying to a God whom I invited *in*, I began praying to Him as though He were outside of me. It's a shift made all too often and all too easily. Think of the last time you prayed. Was your prayer aimed at God way off in heaven, or was it to the Spirit of God who is actually inside you? Maybe there's more to inviting Jesus "in" than that little boy in *Star Wars* pajamas could have ever realized.

That shift, from WITH to IN, changed the whole story. It changed *my* whole story. Contrary to the assumptions we have based on the language we use, God is not merely "out there" or "back then" or "in them." He is *in* you. The question is, do you truly believe that? Do you believe that the same power that spoke the world into existence is in you? Do you live as if the same power with which Jesus healed the sick is in you? If so, then it should not only radically reorder the position of your prepositions in prayer, but also radically reorder your life! Not only is God no longer "out there," and not only is God "in here," but all His power came with Him. His power and presence are not detached from your daily life.

This means that you can pray as if you actually believe it. You can pray, no longer wondering or hoping that God hears, but knowing that He both hears and is *here*! Maybe it's time to start living as if He actually came in, as if He is no longer just with you, but IN you.

The Gift of the Holy Spirit (Acts 2)

What if I told you that for the rest of this week, in every text you send, every email you write, every conversation you have, regardless of whom you are talking to, you have to skip every third word? No matter what, you have to skip every third word. How do you think you would do? How long do you think you would last? How helpful or productive do you think you'd be? It would be awkward if not downright frustrating, right? It would be hard to get across the simplest of ideas.

Consider the following famous American speeches. See how they read with every third word taken out.

> Four score seven years our fathers forth on continent, a nation, conceived Liberty, and to the that all are created.

The Gettysburg Address might not have been nearly as convincing had Lincoln skipped every third word. How about this one?

> I have dream that four little will one live in nation where will not judged by color of skin but the content their character.

You know that it's Martin Luther King's "I Have a Dream" speech, but in this version it reads as if it were written by a caveman! Last one:

> On your ready set go! Dance pro I you know go psycho my new hit. Just sit Gotta jiggy wit.

Not very fresh is it? Clearly, you get the point: Skipping every third word confuses and confounds the clearest and even most compelling things. Yet, for so many Christians, this is how they live their life when it comes to God ... missing the fullness of the power, presence, and significance of the Holy Spirit in their lives.

- God we mostly understand
- Jesus we get
- But the Holy Spirit...?

Even though the Holy Spirit is just as much a part of the Trinity as God the Father and Jesus the Son, we know so little about the Holy Spirit. It's as if we're living with a two-thirds God!

Because the role of the Holy Spirit is often not explored, the power of the Spirit is often not experienced.

Is it possible that you have a two-thirds God?

There are more than a hundred verses about the Holy Spirit in the Bible. Jesus says more about the Holy Spirit than He does about almost all of our hot-button issues combined. In fact, toward the end of His time on earth, before His death and resurrection, Jesus began to prepare His disciples for the reality of the Holy Spirit, the gift of the Holy Spirit. One of those times is found in John 14:16–17:

> "I will ask the Father, and he will give you another advocate to help you and be with you forever—the Spirit of truth. The world cannot accept him, because it neither sees him nor knows him. But you know him, for he lives with you and will be in you."

The New Testament centers around two big gifts from God:

(1) The gift of Jesus
(2) The gift of the Holy Spirit

Both are essential in understanding the New Testament. And ultimately, both are essential in having a relationship with God. The gift of Jesus without the gift of the Holy Spirit keeps the presence and power of God confined to one person (Jesus) in one place (Israel) at one time (His earthly lifetime). The gift of the Holy Spirit simply does not happen without the gift of Jesus. It was Jesus' atoning act of sacrifice on the cross that settled the sin separation between us and God, thus bridging that gap and making a way for a Holy God to inhabit inherently sin-filled people.

The Holy Spirit is central to the story of the New Testament. Everything that happens from Acts 2 to Revelation 22 is directly connected to the power and presence of the Holy Spirit. The same could be said of any moment or movement of God since those days right up to the present. You and I are living in the time and power of IN.

It is fascinating to consider that after 2,000 years of activity, history, and theology, the Holy Spirit still largely remains a mystery. There have been volumes of books written on the Holy Spirit. Churches and denominations have rooted their theology in the Holy Spirit. Yet, to many followers of Jesus today, the gift of the Holy Spirit has gotten lost in a pile of spiritual wrapping paper on the floor.

This was not the case when IN began. Those first followers of Jesus and leaders of the first church were ever aware that the gift of the Holy Spirit had changed everything. The new normal of the Holy Spirit was previously unimaginable. Jesus' disciples were acutely aware of who they were and more specifically who they were not. They saw all that they were doing and saying and the way they were living and knew that this was all much bigger than them.

The same disciples who argued over who would be first in heaven were the first to offer their possessions to those around them who were in need (Acts 2:45; 4:33–35). The same disciples who often misunderstood and missed altogether the teachings of Jesus were the ones who were teaching daily to thousands and thousands of people in the back of the temple (Acts 2:41–42). The same disciples who had botched attempts at miracles in the past were healing people just as Jesus had done (Acts 3:6–10; 5:12–16). The same disciples who had left Jesus as He was being tried and persecuted were suddenly standing before the *same* religious leaders and boldly preaching the death and resurrection of Jesus … and receiving their own punishments for it (Acts 5:17–42). The same disciples who watched their Messiah offer His life for the sake of the world were now offering their lives at the stake of persecution (Acts 7).

Clearly, something had changed. The gift of the Holy Spirit had transformed these followers into leaders. It transformed their view of a kingdom from something of this world, to something not of this world. It transformed the vision they had for their lives. It transformed their relationship with God from something "out there" to someone who is "IN here."

You see, God is a God who gives perfect gifts. He gives you just what you need, just when you need it. We see this throughout the story of the Bible. In the beginning, God gave us life. In the midst of our sin, He gave us the Law and the Prophets. In the desperation of our separation from God, He gave us Jesus. And just when we think that there is no more that God can give.... He gives the Holy Spirit.

The power and presence of the Holy Spirit is not intended to be a great mystery in our lives. The Bible speaks to what the Holy Spirit does *in* our lives and *in* our world. Among many other things, the Holy Spirit brings to our lives:

Comfort (John 14:16)
Counsel (John 16:12–14)
Conviction (John 16:8)
Connection (Rom. 8:26–27)

Jesus said that everything the Father has He gave to Jesus, that He gives all of that to the Holy Spirit, and that the Holy Spirit then in turns gives access to *all* of that to *all* of us. The power and presence of the Holy Spirit is made fully available to every follower of Jesus equally. There aren't some people who get more and some who get less. Some are more open and dependent than others, but God pours out His Spirit freely on *all* followers of Jesus. The Holy Spirit is how God lives IN us and works through us—guiding, guarding, loving, and leading our lives.

What changed the world 2,000 years ago can change your life today. What birthed the revolution of the church can birth a revolution in your soul. What turned unschooled, ordinary people into world-changers can change the perspective and purpose you have for your life. The gift God gave continues to give life to all who enter into relationship with Him. The gift is just as new and just as needed. The gift is as much for you as it was for them.

The Outsider (Acts 9)

I will never forget Justin Griffin-Holtz. He was an imposing force, even for the sixth grade. He had perpetually messy red hair and a mouth overstocked with braces, was built like a lumberjack, and presumably was at my school as a part of the Witness Protection Program, having been a part of some sort of organized crime syndicate at his last school.

I was in fourth grade and, by the laws of the playground, had very little to do with sixth graders. But on this particular day I found myself in a heated game of H.O.R.S.E. with "The Holtz." At some point I made a shot he couldn't make—most likely my famous "one-legged one-hand backwards free throw." In anger, he rebounded his own missed shot and chest-passed it back to me with enough force to knock the wind out of me.

Without thinking, I responded with my second most famous shot: "The one-handed pass to the face of a sixth-grader followed by the 100-yard dash shot." I hit him squarely in the face, causing his nose to bleed and his blood to boil. He immediately began chasing me, shaking the earth with every step. As he reached me and threw me down to the ground, I figured this was the end. It had been a good life, but my life was clearly over ... until over the shrieks and squeals of my own voice, I heard a voice that I knew. It was my brother, Justin. An eighth grader! He and a buddy pulled that prepubescent lumberjack off of me and carried him by the arms across the basketball court right over to the resident recess monitor. That guy never challenged me to a game of H.O.R.S.E. again ... as long as my brother was around.

We all have had our fair share of Justin Griffin-Holtzes—someone God puts in our lives who is the hardest and most challenging for us to love. Bullies. Exes. Bosses. Enemies. We all know how we feel about them ... and many times, how they feel about us. So what would happen if that person became your lab partner, your business partner, your roommate, or your best friend? How would that work? How would that feel?

This was the dilemma facing the first church when they heard that one of the greatest bullies and enemies of the gospel had in fact had a "come to Jesus" moment. For years, Saul of Tarsus had been, as the Bible says, "breathing out murderous threats against the Lord's disciples" (Acts 9:1). He had followers of Jesus regularly imprisoned, had participated in their executions, and was on an all-out mission to extinguish the flame of the gospel from the face of the earth. As a devout and overzealous Jew, he believed that it was his responsibility to replace grace with the old ways before it took root.

In a completely unforeseen turn of events, the enemy of the church became its advocate. The persecutor became the preacher. In one moment, the outsider became the insider. Saul became Paul. And the trajectory of his life and the life of the church would forever change.

Paul was welcomed slowly and cautiously into the church. I mean, it's kind of hard to carpool with the guy who was responsible for the arrest and torture of half of the people in your small group. Within a couple of years Paul had dedicated his life to preaching the gospel and extending the largely localized movement of the church all across the known world. The Great Commission of Jesus given to His disciples in Acts 1:8 of being His "witnesses in Jerusalem, and in all Judea and Samaria, and to the ends of the earth" was ultimately fulfilled by someone who wasn't even there to hear Jesus say it. The outsider, who now had the power and presence of God inside his life, was on a mission to invite other outsiders IN as well.

Up until this moment in the story of the Bible, the church had remained largely ethnocentric. It was a movement of Jews converted to the way of Jesus — people who had both a greater adjustment and a greater appreciation of grace because of a life with the Law.

So along came Paul, the Uber-Jew, initially an outsider to the first church, venturing on a mission to reach other "outsiders." Paul intentionally chose to take the gospel throughout the known world to people-groups that it had yet to reach at home. The Bible calls them Gentiles—just another way of saying "everyone else," all those who weren't Jewish. God chose to use the Ultimate Jewish Insider, an outsider to this new church, to reach those who were outside the church's original focus and mission. When Paul realized that that was God *in* him, he took that message *out* to all of those who never imagined that God was even interested in them. Sometimes it takes an outsider to reach outsiders. It takes someone who has been transformed by grace to offer grace to others. It takes someone who's been wrecked and rebuilt by God to see and speak into the brokenness of this world.

Paul serves as a reflection of what IN does. God enters IN to go OUT. God enters into the most unsuspecting of characters and works out the most amazing stories of faith. He enters into our lives to transform us from the inside out, to send us out into our world. Paul reminds us that there is no one too far outside of the reach of grace—and that the power and message of grace were never meant to stay in, but always to send us out.

All In (Colossians 1)

One of the big values for our family is getting away—from overnight "staycations" in our beautiful city of Chicago, to our annual Christmas-to-New Year vacation with dear friends of ours, to our family summer break. We love to get away with one another. These trips tend to include a lot of midday pajama wearing, minimal showering, hanging out at the beach or playing in the snow (weather dependent), taking walks or naps, and playing lots of family games. A recent family getaway included a four-hour Monopoly game, from which we had to dismiss our five-year-old Gigi twenty minutes in because her level of trash talking was too much even for us!

Elijah had asked me on that trip if I could teach him how to play poker, or as he called it, "pokers." He had heard me talk about playing with a couple guys I know in the city, and he wanted to learn. So I Googled poker for kids and was shocked to find out just how many sites there were dedicated to that. I got out the cards, decided that instead of money we would use pretzels, and set out to teach my son "pokers."

After a few short rounds, just as he started getting the hang of it, he began betting *big*. I tried to be a good dad (even though I was teaching my son to play poker) and told him to play a little more conservatively, but he kept going all in with his pretzels. What's worse is that he kept winning! I tried to inform him that that's not how you play the game. You have to conserve; you have to save. You can't go "all in" every round. But that's a hard lesson to learn when you keep on winning. Within thirty minutes, the boy had all my pretzels and had apparently taught *me* how to play "pokers." Truly, he is his mother's son.

This is a truth that Paul discovered about God. He is a God who goes ALL IN. He always has gone all in and always will. He is a God who doesn't hold anything back and doesn't play it conservatively when it comes to His love for you and for this world. Paul was reflecting and writing on this reality to a group of outsiders in the city of Colossae. In a letter to that church, Paul recounted just how this God has gone all in. He chose to wrap his theology in poetry, what N. T. Wright, in his famous sermon "City on a Hill," called, "One of the first and most beautiful Christian poems." Paul wrote about Jesus that,

> in him all things were created: things in heaven and on earth, visible and invisible, whether thrones or powers or rulers or authorities; all things have been created through him and for him. He is before all things, and in him all things hold together. (Col. 1:16–17)

IN Him, through Him, and for Him, all things were created. He goes ALL IN for *all things*.

Paul is making a big point about Jesus, but he goes on to make an even bigger point—not just about Jesus, but also about you. He says,

> To them God has chosen to make known among the Gentiles [outsiders] the glorious riches of this mystery, which is Christ in you, the hope of glory. (Col. 1:27)

The God who has always gone all in for all things goes all in for you by actually going *in* you. He enters IN. The conclusion to Paul's epic image of the supremacy and centrality of Jesus is that this same Jesus who *by* and *through* and *for* all things are created goes all in with you by choosing to live *in* you through the Holy Spirit. IN is the mystery that has been unfolding since the days of OF. It is now revealed and made known and made possible through the Holy Spirit.

The same power and presence of God that dwelt in Christ Jesus and raised Him from the dead now lives and moves and breathes in you, resurrecting your life and transforming it from the inside out. The Holy Spirit is the fuel to the flame of Jesus that enables you to be a light in this world. Just as the Father sent the Son, the Son sent the Holy Spirit, and the Holy Spirit now sends you into this world. You are no longer alone and no longer dependent on your own power or perspective or will or wisdom. The gift of the Holy Spirit entering into your life is further proof of a God who holds nothing back—a God who goes all IN.

One of the great joys of my role as a father to our son, Elijah, is to teach him to love and respect all the things that mattered to me when I was a kid. That involved playing with all of the original *Star Wars* figures that my mother-in-law kept from her boys' childhood, to watching all the old cartoons that I loved as a kid (which included every single G.I. Joe episode ever made), to learning how to dollie on a skateboard. Some would say that I am reliving my past through him. They are correct, and I make no apologies.

One of my favorite things to do with Elijah as he gets older is to introduce him to the video games I used to play as a kid—the originals, in all their painfully slow glory. He loves *Super Mario Bros.* It's easy enough for him to get and frustrating enough that I still have to walk away from it every now and then. What he loves most about it is when Mario gets the TurboFire Mushroom and is able to run faster and shoot fire (a skill I would love to have in the real world). There's something about that super-charged Mario that makes the game that much more ... super!

In a very real and much less 8-bit way, this is actually what the Holy Spirit does IN our lives. His power and presence make our ordinary, everyday life extraordinary and significant. He makes what is natural somehow supernatural. When He goes all in, it comes out through our lives, enabling us to live much bigger lives than we ever could have dreamed of on our own.

Let's look at how the Holy Spirit does that and what our lives look like when they are supercharged by His presence.

All In with Spiritual Gifts

I remember the first time I ever heard anyone talk about spiritual gifts. I was sitting in the West Balcony of Willow Creek Community Church about 1995. John Ortberg was teaching through the biblical reality of spiritual gifts. It was so revolutionary to me, and yet it made perfect sense! I had spent the better part of my life trying to find ways to use my spiritual gift of teaching, without even knowing what it was. I taught four-and-five-year-olds in Sunday school as a teenager and taught middle school students while in college. Then I was teaching and speaking to high school students at Willow Creek and eventually became a teaching pastor there.

I had been using a gift that God gave me without having a name for it or an understanding of it. I felt a clear and undeniable burden and passion for reaching students and eventually adults. When I began to put the pieces together, I started to see that this passion was actually given to me by God and that it aligned perfectly with the spiritual gifts He had already given me when I entered into relationship with Him! It was He who was inviting me to go ALL IN with these same spiritual gifts and passions that came from Him. They came *from* Him, and they are *for* Him.

Spiritual gifts are one of the most powerful ways that we live out the reality of the Holy Spirit IN us. Those gifts are what God *supernaturally* does with what we *naturally* do. Once again, it is Paul who paints this picture for us. He uses a brilliant metaphor of the body to help us get an idea of the bigger super charged, purpose-filled kind of life that God is inviting each of us into:

> For just as each of us has one body with many members, and these members do not all have the same function, so in Christ we, though many, form one body, and each member belongs to all the others. (Rom. 12:4–5)

This is a very powerful and very intentional metaphor. Paul says that like hands or feet to a body, we are a *part* of something bigger than ourselves. Just like hands and feet and eyes and ears, we have a *part* to play in that body. What we do matters.

But it goes even deeper than that. While it's possible for a body to go on living without a hand or foot or sight or hearing, a hand cannot live without the body, and ears cannot live without the body. The body will not be complete without them, but it will live; yet, none of the parts can live without their connection to the bigger thing that they are a *part* of. Could it be that you are a *part* of a bigger thing, that you have a *part* to play, that you simply will not ever truly live *apart* from the bigger thing that God has invited you into?

There is something that you can give yourself to that is bigger than you. Paul goes on to draw out exactly what that looks like. He traces out the masterpiece that we get to fill in with the beautiful colors of our lives.

> We have different gifts, according to the grace given to each of us. If your gift is prophesying, then prophesy in accordance with your faith; if it is serving, then serve; if it is teaching, then teach; if it is to encourage, then give encouragement; if it is giving, then give generously; if it is to lead, do it diligently; if it is to show mercy, do it cheerfully. (Rom. 12:6–8)

This is how you give yourself to something bigger than you—you use the gifts given to you. Spiritual gifts were the killer app of the first church, and they still are to this day. This is what God does. He gifts everyday, ordinary people like you and me to do things greater than ourselves. God uniquely and distinctly pours Himself into us so that we can do through Him what we could never do on our own.

God's big plan is actually quite small and specific, consistent for all of us and yet unique to each of us. This is what's so beautiful about our God. He gives gifts that are in keeping with whom He created you to be.

All In with Your God-Given Passions

God gives us not only spiritual gifts, but also God-given, Holy Spirit-driven passions. The things that you care deeply about come from a God who cares deeply about you. You may already be aware of your passions. They are the things that you love, that you care about, that you dream about, that you are drawn to without prompting or coercing. For some it's:

- Kids
- Justice / The poor
- Creating something beautiful

- Leading projects
- Serving others
- Teaching
- Entrepreneurialism

Just like spiritual gifts, passions are different for all of us and unique to each of us. What if those things that you really care about were given to you by a God who really cares about you ... and really cares about this world?

Imagine if you could align your spiritual gifts with your God-given passions. What kind of difference do you think you could make in this world? What kind of life would that be?

Somehow we have this notion that serving God is supposed to be hard and difficult and we're not really supposed to enjoy it; we're just supposed to do it ... because that makes God happy. But that's not at all how God designed it. Your spiritual gifts work in tandem with whom God created you to be. In other words *who* you are meant to *be* and *what* you are meant to *do* come from the same place.

All In with Prayer

The idea of "prayer" radically shifted when the Holy Spirit came IN. Prayer throughout the Old Testament and gospel accounts was something that you did to a God who was "out there." Now, through the Spirit, we find that we pray to a God who is "in here." This is a seismic shift in the practice of prayer!

Even though the Holy Spirit changed everything about how we pray, some things remain the same about us. Currently, 55 percent of Americans say they pray every day (Pew Study) ... and yet, if you were to ask them to answer "honestly," most folks feel as if they're not praying right or not praying enough ... or both.

However, prayer remains one of the most central and significant ways that a person connects to God. It is one of the most "spiritual" things you can do ... to talk directly to God. Our access to God through prayer is one of the dynamic ways that separates a relationship with God from a religion about God. But the truth is that anyone who has committed in their heart to pray has found it hard to pray. This is where the Spirit comes in—and in fact, does our job with us and for us.

Romans 8:26–27 says,

> In the same way, the Spirit helps us in our weakness. We do not know what we ought to pray for, but the Spirit himself intercedes for us through wordless groans. And he who searches our hearts knows the mind of the Spirit, because the Spirit intercedes for God's people in accordance with the will of God.

Do you get what Paul is saying there? The Holy Spirit prays *for you*! Even right now as you read this, you are being prayed for by the Holy Spirit. The Holy Spirit is taking the stirring, swirling contents of your soul to the Father. The things that you could never understand yourself, the Holy Spirit already does and takes those parts of you into the very presence of God on your behalf.

I know this firsthand. This past fall, Jeanne and I had a significant health scare with our daughter, Gigi. One afternoon she gradually became very, very sick. We thought that it was a cold or the flu, gave her the right meds, and after some extra cuddles sent her to bed. Within forty-five minutes she came back downstairs crying, saying that she could barely breathe. We called our family doctor, and after fifteen seconds of listening to her breath over the phone, we were directed to go immediately to the nearest emergency room. They believed that Gigi's trachea was blocked and quickly closing up and that if we didn't get her to a doctor within the next hour or so, she might not make it through the night.

A couple of late-night hours in the ER turned into an overnight stay and eventually the better part of the week in Intensive Care. It turns out that Gigi had a very rare infection in her trachea that has a one in a million occurrence rate, but a mortality rate of 1 in 5. The prayers prayed in those sleepless anxious nights in the hospital consisted of very few words. "Oh God …," "Please …," "Help…." These were the best we could do.

Maybe you are familiar with these prayers. Maybe you've found yourself backed into a similar corner with prayer and ... there ... just ... aren't ... any ... more ... words ... to ... say. Isn't it good to know that when you don't know what to say, the Holy Spirit does? To know that, when you are done, the Holy Spirit has only just begun? That the Spirit who is IN you is always praying *for* you and constantly connecting you to the Father who loves you.

Perhaps this is what Paul means in I Thessalonians 5:16 – 18 when he says to "Rejoice always, pray continually, give thanks in all circumstances; for this is God's will for you in Christ Jesus."

We can rejoice because the Spirit who is IN us is praying continually FOR us in ALL circumstances. No matter what. I do not have to muster up the words to pray to a God who's "out there" all by myself and by my own strength. God is already here. The Spirit is already praying. This is what I missed as a boy in the formation of my understanding about prayer — that prayer is about living in a state of awareness of God's presence. In other words, prayer is about living more aware that God is always there.

Prayer is less about a *thing* we do and more about a *way* we live! It is the realization that it is possible for us to live in the constant awareness of God's loving presence in our everyday, ordinary life.

All In with Generosity

But God doesn't stop with spiritual gifts, passions, and prayer. Remember, He is a God who goes all in. God has also given each of us resources. Like gifts and passions, our resources are different from one another's. When you know your spiritual gifts, when you know what you're passionate about, you look at your resources and opportunities differently. These don't become the *end*, but rather the *means* to a bigger end. They no longer become a goal to be achieved, but instead they are things to be used for a greater purpose.

This is how we go all in with the God who is IN us. We lay all the chips of our life on the table and say, "God, if it's all *from* you, then it's all *for* you! I don't want to hold anything back. If you would leverage these things in my life, for something bigger than my life, than have at it!"

I spent the first half of my life fighting God on this one. At some level I was aware that my resources were a gift from God ... and I figured that when I had more, I could eventually take responsibility with my generosity. I gave regularly to God, but it was always the minimum monthly amount—until I had a conversation with David Wills, the president of the National Christian Foundation.

Jeanne and I had asked for the meeting to see if NCF would like to financially help Soul City Church get started. We basically went to ask for money. But David gave us something far better: He gave us vision. He challenged Jeanne and me, in a season where we had leveraged all that we had for God, to consider becoming "reverse givers." The idea is that each year you give back to God more than you gave the year before, so that over time you end up living off of less than you are giving. What?!? Not only did it look as if NCF wasn't going to give Soul City money ... but now their president was asking *us* to consider giving more of our own!

We left there inspired and encouraged. What if we could? What if we could spend a life time of going "all in" with God by giving more and more to Him ... more than ever before, more than we ever dreamed, more than we lived off of?

That vision has actually become our reality. So far, six years after sitting in David's office, we have been able to increase our giving to God every year ... regardless of salary realities. I am seeing for the first time in a lifetime of following Jesus what it really means to go all in with all that I have and all that I am. When we begin to get *who* it's all from, we begin to get *what* it's all for. Our resources are an invitation for us to grow in gratitude and to get better and better at the grace of giving. They provide one more opportunity for me to not hold back from a God who has not held anything back from me!

Conclusion: IN Is Only the Beginning . . .

The beauty and power of this fourth movement in the story of God is that it continues to this day. It does not end in the garden of Eden. It does not end at the birth of Jesus, nor at His death and resurrection.

It is still being written to this day. The ink is still wet. The page is ready to be turned. The pen is in God's hand, and He is offering it to you. God is inviting you to co-author the story of a life lived in the reality of God IN you. This is the story you were born to live. This is the kind of story our world is dying to hear.

Will you choose to know and love and depend and become more aware of the Holy Spirit's power and presence in your life? Will you no longer pray to a God "out there," but live in constant connection with Him? Will you discover your God-given gifts and God-driven passions and align them with the resources that God has entrusted to you? Will you leverage your one and only life for Him? Will you learn to live in the mystery and reality of IN?

4

in the end

Understanding the Story

I'm a huge fan of the director's commentary of movies and TV shows. When Jeanne bought me *The Lord of the Rings Trilogy* for Christmas years ago, I went through and watched *every* minute of commentary and behind-the-scenes footage it had. She didn't see me for three weeks, and when I finally did come out of the basement, I somehow had the ability to speak in Elvish.

I love hearing all the inside information that goes into the final story. I love hearing about the choices made, the directions that story might have gone, the deleted scenes. I love it all. It gives me a better understanding and a deeper appreciation of the greater story.

While there is no director's cut of the Bible, I do hope that this book has given you a better understanding and a deeper appreciation of the story. My hope is that you will look at the Bible differently—that you will be able to recognize the Four Big Movements of the Bible through the Four Small Words: OF, BETWEEN, WITH, IN.

My hope is that you will read the Bible through a whole new lens—a lens that helps you not only to see the bigger story, but to actually see yourself in the story. I hope that you will recognize and have language for the movements of your life and your relationship with God, so that no matter what part of the Bible you are reading or studying, you will have a greater and more personal connection to it. I hope that you will no longer be intimidated by it, but will be fascinated with it instead; that you will be drawn to it; and that you will have a greater desire and ability to share this life-changing, history-altering story with others.

Sharing the Story

Recently, on a Christmas break I set out to begin watching the BBC classic series *Doctor Who*. I remember watching some of the older episodes as a kid and being amazed at how deep the stories were and how cheap the sets and props were. Some good friends of ours from Soul City are huge *Doctor Who* fans and had told me for a while that I would love the program. So, as I sat down to watch Season 1 Episode 1 of the re-launch of the series, I sent Joel and Kate a little text letting them know that it was finally happening, and I asked them to wish me luck! They immediately texted me back in all caps, telling me to "STOP WATCHING SEASON 1. IT'S NOT THAT GREAT. YOU WON'T LIKE IT!!!!" In subsequent texts they replied with the following instructions. (I've reprinted them for you word for word, just as they sent them.)

1. Watch seasons 5—7
2. Jump back to seasons 1—4
3. Jump forward to the 50th anniversary special, then the 2013 Christmas special
4. … and then wait until fall for new episodes with the rest of us.

This is a lot of instruction and a lot of commitment to a show that is already complicated enough to begin with (see The Tardis, Daleks, and Multiple Re-Incarnating Doctors). But I took their orders to heart. In a relatively short amount of time and space, I have become a huge Who fan! In fact, I've gone back and gotten our kids hooked on it. There's nothing like the joy of talking about the fate and location of the planet of Gallifrey with your kids. I call it good parenting!

Unfortunately, Joel and Kate's frantic text message directions are how we so often sound when we try to share the story of the Bible with people who are unfamiliar with it.

- "It's a chronological book … sort of … but not really."
- "*Don't* start in the beginning and try to read it all the way through."

- "Start with the Gospels, then go back ... or forward ... your call."
- You're gonna get bored and lost around Deuteronomy and Leviticus."
- "Save Revelation till later ... much later."

The Bible is already complex and mysterious enough as it is, covering thousands of years, using several languages, employing multiple writing styles, and being broken into two major sections and 66 books. The last thing you and I need to do is make it *more* confusing. Having a "framework" like these Four Small Words helps to bring clarity and simplicity to the mystery and complexity of the Bible. Shining a light on the bigger story has a way of illuminating the smaller stories and all parts in-between. And it makes it much easier to communicate and share with the people whom God has put in your world.

Many people tend not to share their faith with others, not because they don't care about God or their friends, but because they don't feel that they "know enough." They're afraid that they won't be able to answer their friends' questions about God and the Bible.

That's understandable. There are *many* questions we don't or won't have answers to in this life, but that doesn't have to keep you from sharing what you *do* know. Think back to *Doctor Who*. I watched that show, as confusing as it is, because my friends are passionate about it. If I asked them to tell me when the show was first written, or who the head writer is, or who voices the Daleks, they most likely wouldn't be able to answer those questions. (Actually, they probably would.) But in several conversations over the last year, it was their love and enthusiasm that compelled me. *They* loved this show, and I love them, so I will probably love this show. They told me all that I needed to know to get started—and now I am already sharing the show with others.

We share what we care about, whether it's TV shows or restaurants or books or God. When you care about it, you can't help but share it. The *big* prayer I've had for *Four Small Words* from the very beginning is that, through it, God would grow your heart for Him and for the Bible. That your having a greater understanding of the Bible would lead to a greater love for God. That you would share that with whoever needs to hear it. And that you would think of the people whom God has put in your life who may be interested in God, but intimated by the Bible, and share with them what you care about.

My desire and prayer is that you will have greater language for how you share God's story and that it will lead to greater conversations with others. And that by sharing with others, you will care for God more and grow in your relationship with Him and be transformed yet again by this amazing story of God's great love.